TOUCH AND GO

STEVE COPPELL
TOUCH AND GO

WITH BOB HARRIS

WILLOW BOOKS
Collins
8 Grafton Street, London W1
1985

Willow Books
William Collins Sons & Co. Ltd
London · Glasgow · Sydney · Auckland
Toronto · Johannesburg

Photographic acknowledgements
For permission to use photographs reproduced in this
book, the author would like to thank: Colorsport;
County Press; Tommy Hindley; *Liverpool Echo*; and
Bob Thomas

First published 1985

© Steve Coppell 1985

BRITISH LIBRARY CATALOGUING IN PUBLICATION DATA
Coppell, Steve
Touch and go.
1. Coppell, Steve   2. Soccer players
England—Biography
I. Title
796.334′092′4   GV942.7.C6

ISBN 0 00 218146 0

Photoset in Linotron Times Roman by
Rowland Phototypesetting Ltd
Bury St Edmunds, Suffolk
Made and printed in Great Britain by
Billings & Sons Ltd, Worcester

Contents

Foreword by Ron Greenwood MBE

Professional footballers expect that their playing days will be relatively short in comparison to other professions but when one is ended in the middle of a flourishing international career, the realisation must be shattering to say the least. To overcome such an experience demands great character and sense of purpose to face problems of a magnitude that very few people could envisage.

Steve Coppell has proved that he has such qualities to the delight, but not the surprise, of everyone close to him for they are the same attributes he displayed in a career with Tranmere Rovers, Manchester United and England. I selected Steve for his first cap against Italy and for all his subsequent 42 caps with the exception of the last 2 against Luxembourg and Greece while he played under my successor Bobby Robson.

He was, in my terms, a modern type of winger fulfilling every requirement on the right-hand side of the team, whether attacking or defending. No one appreciated him more than his international colleagues both on and off the field and he was always willing to give his intelligent views on any problem that affected the well being of the squad.

The story of Steve Coppell's life so far will be an inspiration to all who read it as to what can be achieved in both triumph and adversity. I feel privileged and honoured to be asked to write the foreword to Steve's story for I know I echo everyone in football when I say Steve Coppell deserves nothing but success wherever his future lies.

1

Injury

It was Friday, 30 September 1983 when the specialist, Jonathan Noble, confirmed my worst fears and told me that, at the age of 28, my playing career was over, wrecked by the continued deterioration of my left knee. It had been finished by a foul tackle committed some 18 months earlier! The tackle had been so unnecessary and futile. The date was Wednesday, 18 November 1981 and the occasion a World Cup qualifying game between England and Hungary at Wembley. The situation had been clear-cut with the Hungarians already having qualified for a place in Spain at the head of Group Four while we needed a draw to beat Romania for the other place.

The Hungarians were content with a couple of days in London, shopping for jeans and *Playboy* magazines, just as long as we did not embarrass them by scoring too many goals. It may sound hard on the paying spectators but once Paul Mariner had taken the pressure off England by scoring the only goal of the match, both sides were happy to play out the remaining time and it was especially apparent in the Hungarians' play. I vaguely remember picking up the ball in the inside right position and running towards the full-back. His name was Josef Toth, a raw-boned 30-year-old and not unlike Norman Hunter in looks. I had played against him once before, in 1978 when we beat them 4–1, and he was the sort of defender I felt comfortable playing against – big, strong and square rather than the nimble, nippy type who could match me for pace.

I saw Toth diving in, almost as if in slow motion. I had time to think that I would knock the ball down the line and go past him before kicking it into the middle. The only other coherent thought I had in the next moments was of my knee exploding as if someone had let off a firework inside it. It was almost as if I had lost consciousness until the roar of the crowd gradually pierced my mind. I reached down to touch my leg which felt as if it was on fire and, thankfully, found that it was all in one piece – or so I thought at the time.

The tackle had taken place right by the touchline and I crawled off on my hands and knees. By the time our physiotherapist reached me the substitute, Tony Morley of Aston Villa, was already stripping off in preparation to take my place and I was lifted to my feet and limped back to the dug-out. The team doctor, Vernon Edwards, looked it over but I was able to walk back to the dressing room unaided. I had taken quite a clout and it hurt like hell though there was no indication of just how serious an injury it was even when it swelled up like a balloon. Dr Edwards strapped it up tightly and gave me the usual anti-inflammatory tablets to take.

After the game I simply carried on as normal, attending a Courage's sponsorship function at the conference centre at Wembley before turning down the offer of a room at the complex's hotel in preference to driving myself back home to Manchester up the motorway. It was not false bravado but just that I had never had a mechanical injury before and so did not realise the problems that they can cause. I kept telling myself that everything was fine while the increasing pain kept telling me differently. I even put down my failure to sleep to the normal post-match high as I lay in bed re-running the game and the tackle in my mind. I had barely closed my eyes before I had to get up to go to Old Trafford for treatment the next day but, by then, the knee was so puffy that it was difficult for anyone to diagnose the extent of injury and it was guessed that I had strained ligaments at the side of the knee.

If only that was all it had been! There was nothing else to do but go home and rest until a proper examination could be made. Toth's tackle began to take on more significance and I was keen to see a re-run of the incident on video. As it turned out my visual recall of it was totally different from the tape I finally saw after my retirement. I thought that the Hungarian had hit me in the back of the left leg which had twisted awkwardly because the boot studs were firmly fixed in the lush Wembley turf. The cameras showed, in fact, that it was my right leg which was planted and that Toth came straight through from the front, spinning my left leg up in the air as though I was Alan Pascoe taking the first hurdle at Crystal Palace.

To this day I cannot believe that I sustained such a serious injury from the tackle. As the then Chairman of the Professional Footballers'

Association I knew only too well how often knee injuries finished a career – as many as 15 a season – but in almost every case it was the planted leg that was injured with the free leg escaping because it could ride the blow. Call it morbid curiosity if you like but I still have the video recording of the tackle and looking at it even now I still cannot understand it.

Obviously I do not harbour a great deal of affection for Josef Toth and on the night of 30 September, over a year later, I could cheerfully have strangled him. However, I suppose I must accept some of the responsibility myself for being so careless as to be caught by such a clumsy foul, especially when I was fully aware of the man and what he was like. On the two occasions I played against him he adopted such scare tactics as niggling, pushing and generally trying to dominate the play. I have always thought that big, tough brutes like him have no place in a good team and are indicative of an inadequate side with a lack of quality players.

The devious sort were always a greater source of concern to me than the lumbering giants but, despite stories to the contrary, British football is thankfully short of them. Our so-called hard men are tough but fair. When they do overstep the mark it is usually patently obvious to everyone and especially to the match officials. Certainly we do not hold a candle to some of our continental cousins in this department, especially the Italians and the Spanish. My first experience of these added difficulties came in the 1977–78 season playing for Manchester United in the European Cup Winners' Cup when, after beating the top Dutch side Ajax in the first round, we came up against the Italian giants Juventus. It was the classic confrontation between two famous sides and it guaranteed that the first leg at Old Trafford would be a 56,000 sell-out.

We had a reputation at the time for being a fast, attacking side and this was obviously not lost on the Italians. Our manager Tommy Docherty warned us beforehand of what the style of play would be like. He told us that they would go through every trick they knew in the game plus a few recent ones of their own invention. As a forward who always enjoyed running at full-backs I thought I knew most of the defenders' methods of stopping us. Of course I was aware of the Italians' notoriety but I was hardly trembling in my shoes at the prospect of playing against them. In fact I was quite looking forward to coming up against an international defender of Marco Tardelli's reputation. It was not long before our opening assault on the Juventus goal brought our first corner and, not being the biggest player on the park, I took up my usual nuisance station by the near upright. Tardelli followed me and marked me as closely as I have ever been marked – by standing on my foot and digging in the studs on his heel. Just to emphasise the point he twisted his boot a little more and I reacted instinctively by pushing him away.

Tardelli promptly fell to the ground clutching whichever part of his anatomy he imagined I had struck. Needless to say the referee saw his extravagant gesture and came racing over. Tardelli made the most of it by demanding protection – from me! I was in agony and suddenly I became the villain of the piece and was being lectured about my conduct. Tardelli did not finish there, either. Because we were so much on top in that first leg I was constantly backing into him and whenever I did I felt a sharp stab of pain in my side. I realised that he was pinching me! Like all our attackers, I was black and blue by the end of the game.

In common with most British players, I find the spitting and hair pulling abhorrent but, incredibly, Juventus managed to surpass themselves in the return leg with something new and even more sinister. I can take it only as a compliment that, having been followed around Old Trafford by Tardelli, I was assigned to the care of Claudio Gentile in the second leg when despite our first leg pressure, we were defending a lead of a single goal only. It was a wet night far removed from the sort of weather that holidaymakers usually enjoy on the Adriatic coast. The greasy pitch was tailor-made for the typical British sliding tackle and as I went skidding in alongside Gentile, he belied his name by firmly grasping my testicles! I completely froze, more from shock at the deed rather than from any pain involved. Ever since that tackle I have physically winced every time I have seen Gentile on television.

However, Italy, like Argentina under Menotti, cleaned up their act to everyone's advantage especially their own. I must say that I came to regard Tardelli and Gentile in the highest esteem. They were hard and uncompromising but both could use the ball beautifully and when the Italians won the World Cup in Spain in 1982 I thought that Tardelli was one of the outstanding players of the competition. Strangely, I made my international début against the Italians and, after my early experiences against Juventus, I feared the worst. Although both Tardelli and Gentile played, I was marked by Zaccarelli in the first half and then by Cuccureddu in the second. I was convinced that we had forced the Italians to change their tactics by our performance but I must add that far from it being another Juventus it was more like that game with Hungary in which I was tackled by Toth. Italy had already qualified for the World Cup finals in Argentina and we needed to score far more than the two goals we beat them by. A similar volatile Latin temperament is often evident over in South America as well. The full range of fouls and retaliatory acts has been vividly recorded by the cameras over the years and it has led to a strange compromise among the South American referees. I saw this at first hand on my first England tour to Brazil, Argentina and Uruguay in 1977. We had gone over there feeling none too hopeful only to surprise everyone by holding the powerful Brazilians to a goalless draw in the massive Maracana Stadium in Rio under the watchful eye of the late Les Cocker while manager Don Revie was away on other business in the United Arab Emirates.

The result gave us all a boost, even those on the sidelines like myself. We needed that and more in Argentina where we played the home side for the first time since Sir Alf Ramsey had called them 'animals' after captain Antonio Rattin had been sent off in a World Cup Finals match at Wembley in 1966. There was also that small matter of the Falkland Islands adding a little spice to the affair and to say that the atmosphere was tense would be to understate the case. England played it fairly and tight and none more so than Leeds United defender Trevor Cherry who was given the difficult task of marking Daniel Bertoni, a job he did superbly without once overstepping the line into the illegal area. Ironically Bertoni's only touch of any significance was when he scored from a free kick to equalise Pancho Pearson's surprise early goal for England.

Bertoni's frustration at his team's ineffectiveness gradually increased until he could take no more and, after Cherry had again denied him space, he turned round and punched him on the mouth. No acting was needed in this instance as Cherry was lying on the ground with blood streaming from his mouth; one tooth knocked out and another split clean in half. The South American referee consulted his South American linesman and, quite correctly, sent Bertoni off the field for violent conduct. Then, to everyone's absolute astonishment, he also showed the red card to the blameless Cherry who went off to a barrage of coins and other missiles. It was explained to us later that the referee had made this outrageous decision to ensure that no riot broke out in the infamous Bon-Bon Stadium. It seems that this was quite normal and that if a home player was sent off a member of the opposing team had to go as well.

Cesar Menotti did a good job in helping clean up the Argentina team, just as Enzo Bearzot had done with his Italian World Champions, but what a pity no one has been able to do the same thing with Spanish football. Whenever I played against a Spanish side they seemed more concerned with breaking up moves than creating them. There was rarely any intention of playing football and, even though they possessed the traditional Latin skills, they were mainly concerned with fouling anyone who threatened them. If they are to fulfil their potential it must rest in their own hands. It is success at any price and until someone sets the example of making good football succeed their game will be ruled by violence and thuggery. Let us hope that Terry Venables' success with Barcelona is an example the rest of Spanish football will follow.

Happily it is not a problem in the Football League. There was no secret about my injury yet no one ever tried to take unfair advantage of it or at least not to my knowledge. I can honestly say that I am on speaking terms with every full-back I have played against in Britain. Although we have gained a reputation around the world for playing very physical football it is invariably conducted at a very fair and sporting level. Playing on the wing you tend to come up against the same full-backs season after season, and you build up a rapport so that it becomes almost like a club within the game. Players like Joey Jones, Alan Kennedy, John Bailey and others would come over in a quiet moment and ask after mutual friends. The likelihood of one of those players deliberately trying to put me out of the game was remote to say the least.

Obviously some players are tougher than others. The names of

Graham Roberts, Remi Moses, Graeme Souness and Paul Miller come
to mind as recent examples but the hardest side I ever played against
was Don Revie's Leeds United. They were undoubtedly a very good
side; they could play football but they were also extremely physical
and everyone was wary of going into a 50–50 ball against any of them.
In those days Peter Storey, Tommy Smith and Norman Hunter were
known as the 'hard men'. I remember Norman with great affection as
he was a delightful character off the field and that probably influenced
me in one of my early games against Leeds when I could have had
Norman sent off. He was booked for a late tackle against me and, just
a couple of minutes later, he sent me tumbling again. Norman could
see the referee striding purposefully towards us and he urgently bent
over and said: 'For God's sake, Steve, get up.' I know that if I had
made a fuss about it he would have been on his way to an early bath.

To Norman's obvious relief and the doubting referee's satisfaction I
jumped to my feet only to walk straight into a severe dressing down
from my team-mate Tommy Jackson for not behaving professionally.
He maintained that I should have stayed down and rolled about a bit
which would have had Norman sent off and reduced the powerful
Leeds side to ten men. I did not because it is not in my nature to do
that. That isn't to say I haven't been on the ground for a bit longer
than necessary at times but I have never done it to get a fellow
professional into trouble and only to gain a bit of breathing space when
we have been under a lot of pressure or if I have been exhausted
after having rushed down that right wing a few times. The most
spectacular-looking fouls do not usually hurt at all and British players,
generally, are no good at feigning injury. Not only do the fans dislike
it but so do most players and few British referees will be fooled by it.

Unfortunately no unity of purpose exists between British and Continental referees and they often seem to operate along different lines. I
have always had great respect for our referees but in recent years they
have become stricter and more aloof from the players. There are too
many bookings, not for dangerous fouls but for minor infringements
such as outbursts at the officials in the heat of the moment. It is a pity
they are not encouraged to mix with the players a little more. Players
and officials cannot be separated as black and white, there must be
shades of grey. If referees chatted with the players after matches or,

better still, trained with them, the game would benefit immediately. Referees would get to know the individuals, understand what makes each one tick and decide whether they are cynical or just occasionally lose their tempers.

Personally I have no complaints about British referees. I never had too much trouble and when I was forced to quit the game I received some very sympathetic letters and telephone calls from officials. The deterioration of my knee and my eventual retirement owed nothing to bad officiating or to dirty play from my fellow professionals in the Football League. Apart from Toth I had only myself to blame.

Hindsight is a dangerous thing but I wish now that I had taken specialist advice on the night of the initial injury against Hungary and that I had pulled out of games I was not really fit enough to play in. There have been many rumours that I was forced to play by Manchester United manager Ron Atkinson but none of them is true. No one forced or even tried to persuade me to play when I was not fit. They always asked me if I was ready to play and it was only my own stubbornness which made me go out when my knee was not right. Nor can you blame the England medical officials on the night of the Hungary match for there were no obvious indications that it was cartilage trouble. There were none of the usual signs, it did not click, it did not lock and though it hurt, I still had full range of movement.

The physiotherapists, doctors and surgeons can only help once the player has decided something is wrong and I had not had too many injury problems from which to gain experience, in fact I once had a four-year spell with Manchester United without missing a single game, even though I suffered the usual minor ailments. Players tend to ignore these and struggle on despite them but it is not always the best thing to do and I should have learned my lesson at the start of the 1981–82 season. It was an unhappy start to the new campaign altogether when our likeable physiotherapist Jimmy Headridge collapsed during training. Everyone thought he was fooling around but sadly he had died by the time they reached the hospital.

Ron Atkinson had taken us to a pre-season tournament in Aberdeen and while playing against West Ham United I strained the ligaments in my right ankle. It was a nagging pain, similar to toothache but I kept going because I wanted to impress the new manager. I played, and played badly, but there were other injuries in the team and I did not want to complain. I struggled through nine games and just when I felt that I was getting it right and coming back to form the manager dropped me. It was hard to take, especially as the game was against our old rivals Manchester City. As it happened I came on as substitute for Garry Birtles and was brought back and scored in the next game against Birmingham City at Old Trafford. However, I made myself a promise that I would never play again when I was unfit. It scarcely ranks as one of the great pledges of our time!

When the 1982 World Cup Finals in Spain came along I was in trouble again but this time it was the injured knee causing me problems and they were bad enough for there to be doubts over whether or not I should go to Bilbao at all. I managed to satisfy Ron Greenwood and myself that all would be well but it was soon to prove otherwise. I was forced to miss the vital game against Spain and both Dr Vernon Edwards and physiotherapist Fred Street recommended I should see David Dandy in Cambridge for arthroscopy on the damaged cartilage.

I was ready to go there on the day I returned from Spain to get it over and done with but when I arrived at Old Trafford I discovered that the manager Ron Atkinson was still in Spain along with club physio Jim McGregor who was looking after the Irish team. I asked Les Olive, the club secretary, to get in touch with Ron to obtain permission to have matters arranged and it was four more days before I packed my pyjamas and headed south with our chief coach Tony Collins.

However, when we arrived it was not as simple as that for David Dandy was not only a very busy man but was also heading off on a well-earned holiday. I was desperate, the season was only eight weeks away and I knew from other players' experiences that it was going to be a six-week job just getting fit enough to train again. Fortunately Dandy relented and in a couple of days I was back in the Cambridge clinic again and what is more, in good company as Scotland's John Wark had also come back from the World Cup in Spain to face an operation. We even managed to slip out to a couple of local pubs for three or four pints. It was a good, if unusual way to relax at such a crucial time. The next day the operation was performed and I was ready to resume my career – or so I thought.

David Dandy had not earned his world-wide reputation lightly. A mere five and a half weeks after the operation I played against Birmingham City at Old Trafford in the first game of the season on 28 August and, what is more, I scored. Indeed I played 29 First Division games that season: 8 times in the Milk Cup; 4 times in the FA Cup; twice in the UEFA Cup and even 2 friendlies against Bolton and my old club Tranmere. I also played twice for England and, in all, scored 13 goals including 8 on the road to Wembley in the Milk Cup. However, the problems continued and I regularly made the 8-hour round trip to Cambridge.

The crazy thing was that I did not have a bad season even though I was playing from match to match with little or no training as my knee would not stand up to that sort of pressure. I was seeing out the season, waiting for it to end so that I could go into hospital to have a second operation, and yet because I had to use my football brain instead of my heart, lungs and speed, I played some of the best football of my career. Before every game I was pumped full of anti-inflammatory drugs which played havoc with the lining of my stomach but the best painkiller was simply playing. I have spoken to other injured sportsmen who agree that physical exercise is the best drug. Either you forget about the pain or else it fades into the background. It is only afterwards when the pain returns that you wonder how you got through it all.

The end finally came in a League match against Sunderland at Roker Park. It was to be my last game. The date was 4 April 1983 and from the moment Iain Munro tackled me I knew something had gone. It was a perfectly fair challenge but I landed awkwardly and knew immediately I was in serious trouble. To make matters worse Lou Macari had gone off with an injury after only ten minutes and I more or less had to stay on or we would have been down to ten men. I stood out on the wing doing little more than making up the numbers for the last half an hour before hobbling off to the dressing room on the final whistle.

The semi-finals of the FA Cup were coming up in a few weeks and I felt choked in the certain knowledge that I would miss it. I could not even face going into the players' lounge for a drink after that Sunderland game and all I wanted was to escape to the peace of the team coach. With my leg heavily strapped, in pain and limping badly I went out of the dressing room only to be stopped by a sympathetic David Meek, the respected football correspondent of the *Manchester Evening News*, who was with other northern-based journalists on the look-out for after-match quotes.

I explained to David I did not want to talk just then and that I would speak to him later. That obstacle clear I struggled on towards the coach, asking the youngsters waiting for autographs to excuse me. Suddenly someone grabbed me by the shoulder and spun me round. It turned out to be a journalist named Doug Weatherall who stuck his face close to mine and began effing and blinding at me, telling me I had no right to barge through the kids and that when the Press asked questions they were entitled to answers. He was literally purple in the face and his veins were sticking out of his neck. In fact I have always been flattered by the attention of kids and other autograph hunters while I have always found time to talk to football writers, enjoying the opportunity to put over my own point of view and to talk about the game in general. Weatherall's behaviour was inexcusable and I often wonder if he remembers his conduct that night after my last game of football.

Needless to say I was in an awful mood on the way back to Manchester and when I got home to Cheshire I told my long-suffering wife Jane that I would need another operation and that I was beginning to fear the very worst. Certainly I had some sort of premonition because, for the first time in my life, I began to keep a diary of the daily events during what I realised then would be a critical period of my football career, if not my life. Keeping a diary was also very therapeutic, almost like having my own private confessional.

2

Touch and Go

Wednesday 13 April. Nine days after the Sunderland game. Though not normally a superstitious person, I found myself hoping that the date was not significant as I went to the BUPA Hospital in Manchester for exploratory arthroscopy.

It was reassuring to see the club physiotherapist Jim McGregor before I was put to sleep. When I came round Jim was still there and he told me that when the specialist, Jonathan Noble, had opened me up he had immediately confirmed my suspicion that there was a tear in the posterior section of the medial cartilage. Closer inspection had also revealed that there was a large piece of cartilage lodged there which he had removed.

Thursday 14 April. I woke up early and lay on my bed feeling uncomfortable, sorry for myself and totally useless until the arrival of Noble at 7.30 a.m. relieved the boredom. He took the time to tell me exactly what he had done and even went to the trouble of drawing diagrams to show me the various stages of the problem, starting with a normal healthy joint and tracing its deterioration from the fateful tackle in November 1981 until this last operation. Considering my doubts before the operation, it all sounded like good news and I began to perk up enormously. However, Noble then went on to explain that the cartilage is there for a reason, namely to stop the bones rubbing together. These bones, he said, should be hard and shiny rather like ball bearings, but since the tackle and the damage to the meniscus, one section of the bone had been rubbing against the other, causing a great deal of harm. Far from the bone being hard and shiny, it was dull and the surface resembled those photographs of the moon's surface. Noble was completely honest and told me that he envisaged me playing at my present level for a further two seasons with intermittent problems and then, after that, it would all be downhill. Although one's initial reaction to hearing news like that is that it must be wrong, I immediately accepted it. I went home later that day and my wife Jane was initially happy because the news was better than we had hoped and even when I told her of the inevitable problems to follow, she was still typically bright and optimistic about the whole thing.

Friday 15 April. I had another appointment with Noble and he said how pleased he was with my knee and set me the target of getting fit for the FA Cup Final if United are successful against Arsenal tomorrow and, if not, to rest it until next season. He told me to start with very gentle quadricep exercises and even the prospect of those felt good. I headed back to the club, taking with me a souvenir of the operation – a little jar containing the pieces of removed cartilage. Understandably everyone at the club was preoccupied with tomorrow's match but the manager, Ron Atkinson, took the time to ask me how I was.

Saturday 16 April. The day started well and the leg felt good. A university friend, Brian Barwick, who works for BBC *Grandstand*, had made arrangements for me to watch United's semi-final against Arsenal from the comfort of the BBC television studios. Although you don't get any of the atmosphere that you do when watching such an important game as this live I thought it sensible as I can't bend my leg 90 degrees and sitting in the Villa Park stands would have been very cramped, not to mention the fear of getting my knee knocked.

My thoughts were mixed as I sat and watched the two teams warming up. A little voice inside my head kept telling me that it would be better if the lads were beaten and then I could have my three months' rest without feeling any pressure or missing a final. But once the game got under way that thought was drowned by the possibility of all my mates losing to a poorer team in such a vital game when Arsenal scored the opening goal through Tony Woodcock.

Two fabulous goals from Bryan Robson and Norman Whiteside capped a tremendous fight back and the lads were through to Wembley. Then that little voice kept telling me that I now had a chance to give it a try but, at the same time, I decided to be completely honest about it with both the club and myself and to admit if I was not fit enough to do the team and me justice.

Sunday 17 April. A pleasant, restful Sunday. Light exercises went well, the leg felt much improved and I was even walking better. A very encouraging sign for Wembley and my future!

Monday 18 April. The improvement was not only maintained but also confirmed by Noble. The stitches are due to come out – it is just five days – and he was as delighted as I. He told me I could start swimming on Wednesday and even begin light training the following Monday. There was hardly any pain and little discomfort and I arranged to see him again on Friday.

Tuesday 19 April. My leg felt terrible. I had planned to go to Goodison Park and watch the lads play Everton but I soon changed my mind and decided to take things very easily. I tentatively removed the bandage from around the knee and noted that there was a lot more fluid than yesterday so I put the leg up and rested. I was in bed by 8.30 p.m. and needed a couple of tablets to ease the throbbing.

Wednesday 20 April. The operation was a week ago today and though there was less fluid on the leg than yesterday, it still felt sore. After feeling so good on Monday it seemed all wrong to have this relapse and, try as I might, I could not think what I had done to bring this about. I had kept in touch with Jim McGregor and he was very concerned when I told him how red and hot it had looked the previous night and that it was still aching painfully. Jim was taking a well-earned day off but left his planned afternoon in the garden to come and have a look for himself. He was so worried that he even took the precaution of ringing Noble who was anxiously awaiting Jim's verdict. It seemed that it was symptomatic of a severe post-operative problem. Jim took one look and feared that the swelling coupled with the redness was a sign of infection. Within 45 minutes we were in Salford Royal Hospital for an appointment with Noble.

To test the amount of inflammation, Noble used his lips, sensitive to half a degree of heat, to conclude that the knee was not overly hot though both Jim and I, using our untutored palms, had thought otherwise. Noble explained that the heightened colour was nothing more than the antiseptic solution used to clean the area before the operation and had absolutely nothing to do with the condition of the knee. However, he had no explanation for the 'effusions'. He insisted that it was only temporary and if the knee was not used at all everything would be fine, including my chances of playing in the Cup Final.

I was bandaged from ankle to crotch, given a pair of crutches and told to report back on Friday. Jim was naturally a little embarrassed by his mistake but took it all in his stride. Having already written off his afternoon, he then wrecked any plans he had for the evening by driving me back to Cheshire.

Thursday 21 April. My leg was sore and uncomfortable and the only way to ease it was to lie around and do nothing but watch television, with the result that I am fast becoming an expert on snooker.

Friday 22 April. Another restless, uncomfortable night was somewhat relieved by the knowledge that I would be leaving the house for a while, seeing Noble and having that restricting, bulky bandage removed. It was very pleasant just driving to the Cliff in a borrowed automatic car and there was even time to have lunch with Jim McGregor before we left.

However, instead of taking the bandage off, Noble told me that it would be best not to move the leg all weekend and he strapped me up in a leg-length back splint. Having gone into the hospital on crutches just to impress Noble and show him what a good boy I had been, I found myself having to use them for real. After leaving the hospital I headed reflectively to Manchester city centre and the north-west premiére of the World Cup film *G'Olé*. It brought back some good memories and the close-ups of the players inspired me towards preparing myself for the renewed target of the Cup Final. It was all very well while I was sitting there in the dark but as I got up to leave I remembered that the inflammation had slowed my recovery and that time was getting short.

Saturday 23 April. Wave the flag. It was St George's Day and to mark the occasion I could feel a distinct improvement . . . I was even able to wiggle my toes. The monotony was broken because it was match day and United were playing Watford. I joined in the ritual pre-match meal at the Midland Hotel and watched Laurie Cunningham and Ashley Grimes score the goals in a 2–0 win. But it was hard to feel involved. In fact I already felt like an outsider and was sure I must already be sounding like an embittered ex-professional who goes around moaning about the lack of characters in the game. At least my splint provoked a little sympathy.

Sunday 24 April. More improvement. For the first time in a week I could perform straight leg lifts with my toes pulled in. I stepped up the exercises confident in the knowledge that Noble would give the OK for the splint to come off but he dashed my hopes by telling me to keep it on until Tuesday, adding that I would feel the benefit of the extra 24 hours in a couple of weeks.

Monday 25 April. I walked to the post box twice! Both my leg and my confidence were on the up and up. Another new avenue opened when I returned a call from Paddy McGrath. He wanted to tell me about a certain Mr Millwood who had apparently cured Sir Stanley Matthews when he was on the brink of retiring and then helped him play until he was 50. The story goes that such is Sir Stan's gratitude, he still phones Millwood each week from all over the world. There was, however, one snag which was that he was in his eighties and no longer taking on new patients. But the fact that I played on the wing, like Sir Stan, should count in my favour according to Paddy.

Tuesday 26 April. At last Tuesday and my appointment with Noble. What was more the telephone rang and it was Paddy to tell me that Mr Millwood would see me that same afternoon. Mr Millwood was our first stop and he began the examination by telling me that the splint was useless and that I was to take it off. I was very nervous when he examined the knee for I had not bent it for five or six days and tensed the muscles to protect it. He sensed my apprehension and told me to relax which he helped me do with his practised fingers. Far from hurting, he announced that it was out of balance before suddenly exclaiming: 'There I've got it moving, I knew I would, but not so quickly.' I couldn't really share his excitement because I had just relaxed. He then asked me to walk around the room a couple of times and, again, it was logical that it should feel easier because I had not walked unaided for almost a week. A little more manipulation and he confirmed that the balance had been restored.

I began to wonder just how he achieved an OBE when he reprimanded me for being 'useless' and a 'dope' because I was awkwardly trying to copy an exercise which involved sitting on the edge of a table and swinging my leg. The old man did it effortlessly while I was very awkward. However, at the end of it all he announced that all would be well in a few weeks, he would see me next Thursday and that would be £15 please. I got a special rate as it is normally £20 for the first visit. Only time will tell whether he has any healing knowledge or is a quack. If he is a con-man then he is certainly a good one.

From there it was straight on to Noble who was nowhere near as pleased with my progress. There is still some fluid around the joint and he showed his reservations by telling me to take the splint home with me just in case. He also instructed me to take things very easily and to concentrate on rebuilding my wasted quad muscles. He seemed to be suggesting that I must not expect too much. Was he trying to tell me something?

Wednesday 27 April. I gave the day over almost entirely to exercise beginning with that one of Mr Millwood's. Then it was on to the club for body work, plus quads before finishing up at the Lymm Health Club where I had a strenuous session that left me feeling in a better mental state but through it all the knee felt uncertain and sore around the affected area.

Thursday 28 April. After another session at the club I kept my appointment with Millwood. He manipulated the joint for a full 40 minutes in what seemed like a trance. I sat there wondering whether he was a complete fraud and that feeling was not helped when I told him I could not see him on Saturday because I was going to Norwich with the team and he said that I shouldn't be playing because I wasn't fit! But I must admit that the knee felt freer and that effect lasted all night.

Saturday 30 April. Three weeks to go before the final against Brighton and I was in pain all day. It hardly mattered that the team had only drawn 1–1 because I had the same pain that I had had before the operation at the back of the knee. It dug in so badly that I did no exercises at all.

Sunday 1 May. I woke up tentatively. There was no severe pain but I took no chances and had an extremely easy day.

Monday 2 May. The lads are flying off to Spain tomorrow and I went with them to the Hilton at Gatwick and, for no particular reason, got absolutely plastered. The manager came down to complain about the noise at around 3.30 a.m. but after he had gone back to bed our behaviour grew progressively worse. I vaguely remember trying to toss Ray Wilkins's shoes onto a huge model aeroplane that was suspended from the ceiling in the foyer before finally crawling into bed at around 6 a.m.

Tuesday 3 May. Suffered all the usual regrets when, after an hour's deep sleep, I crawled out of bed to go back to Manchester on the empty team bus. I am sure I wouldn't have passed a Breathalyser test had I driven back but I arrived safe enough to keep my appointment with Noble who told me that the fluid around the knee may well be a permanent fixture from now on. Apart from that he noticed a marked improvement and gave the go-ahead to start running and to use weights in my recovery programme.

Wednesday 4 May. Woke up to find a letter from the club telling me that I could take one guest free to the Cup Final and, if I wanted, two more at £150 each. We had to pay that to take our guests to the Milk Cup Final. The manager explained in his letter that there was no money to be made from the competition. I thought this very sad. Why should a youngster like Norman Whiteside have to pay so much so that his parents could watch him play in the Cup Final? The lads are away until Friday and they are sure to be angry about it when they return. It sent me into my day's training with renewed zest starting with a swim and ending with a Jacuzzi. Fingers crossed that the day's work would bring no reaction.

Thursday 5 May. No apparent reaction, just a little irritation. Kept training to a minimum in the morning so that I could celebrate my Dad's birthday.

Friday 6 May. Today I started cycling, which I intend to keep up, and jogging. The running was not as successful as I would have wished and Jim McGregor said it was because I would not 'let go'. He is right but I will not let go because the leg is simply not strong enough at this stage.

Saturday 7 May. I jogged a little more this morning, stopping when I started limping too badly. The cycling was much more successful because there was less pressure put on the knee.

Sunday 8 May. I finally had to accept that Steve Coppell would not figure in the Cup Final when I was told that to have any chance of selection I would have to play for the reserves a week tomorrow. I couldn't even play golf, never mind football! I had planned to caddy at Lou Macari's golf tournament but arrived too late. I was almost tempted into playing and even went so far as a practice shot. No good at all. It put an enormous strain on my left leg and I made a mental note that I would have to limit my golf activity as well.

I settled for a walk instead but even that was a problem after half an hour and I quit for the sanctuary of the 19th.

With the Cup Final no longer a realistic target, my aim is now to get as fit as possible despite my handicap, even to the extent of doing daily quad exercises through the summer to build up my leg muscles.

I arrived home that night to learn that Manchester United were going to allow us to take three guests to the Final in exchange for having 'Sharp' advertisements on the open-top bus when we drive through Manchester to our civic reception. Considering that the agreement is probably worth a five-figure sum there is no doubt as to who is getting the best deal.

Monday 9 May. I told Jim McGregor that I had more or less made up my mind that I had no chance of making Wembley especially as the jogging went badly again. He encouraged me to give it one more day and to try running, as increased pace is often easier than jogging. It seemed pretty futile and I was in just the right frame of mind for an argument with Atkinson about the number of players entitled to those three free guests. He had said 16 but we claimed that we had a legitimate squad of 20. No one would give way and the players left saying that they would sell the three guest tickets for £150 each and organise their own trip to Wembley.

Tuesday 10 May. The expected trial run turned out to be a non-event as I could jog a couple of laps only and, without the reserve match or Wembley being mentioned, it was decided that I should concentrate on quads only from now until mid-June. I passed on the decision to Noble at our afternoon meeting and he seemed quite pleased as he felt that I would still have difficulties in the future and that I should be thinking in terms of what I should do when they arose. Should I retire or should I have the complete cartilage removed for the sake of another year's football at the risk of being more disabled later in life? His words struck home but I felt determined to do everything in my power to delay the judgement day.

I could see a number of avenues of self-help:

1) I could lose weight gradually over a long period so that my strength would not be sacrificed but the amount of pressure on my knee would be reduced.

2) A change in diet. There are a large number of books claiming that such changes can help arthritis. This may be a load of rubbish but I feel I owe it to myself to study them and form my own opinion.

3)   I could continue with my straight leg quadricep exercises to try and make my legs and relevant muscles really strong.

These alternatives were going through my head as I attended the Tranmere Rovers Centenary Dinner and, as if to confirm my decision to abandon all thoughts of playing again this season, my leg ached all night.

Wednesday 11 May. Experienced a strange burning sensation behind my knee while doing a circuit at the Health Club and immediately cut down on the exercises.

Thursday 12 May. The discomfort was still there and I kept to my word. No work.

Friday 13 May. An ominous day and date and when I went to Old Trafford to sort out my mail I discovered that Bill Park, the radiologist who had looked after my knee in Shrewsbury, had died on 22 April. I did not know him well but I felt very depressed by the news.

Saturday 14 May. Went to watch Rochdale play Hull City. They lost 3–1 and clearly my old club-mate Jimmy Greenhoff has taken on one hell of a job. I was struck by the contrast of Rochdale one week and Wembley the next. Football is a humbling game and I wonder whether I will be in Jim's position one day.

Sunday 15 May. First exercise for days when I did a little gardening. All went well but Jim McGregor, Jonathan Noble and I decided together that I should do nothing more until after my holiday in July.

Monday 16 May. It seems that word about my availability has been circulating on the grapevine and it looks as though I may become something of a socialite. Neil McFarlane, Minister for Sport, has invited me to the Savoy Hotel in London to attend a dinner in honour of an important politician from Kuwait who is over here to discuss the possibility of sportsmen from Britain going over there to train and advise. An excellent evening was ensured when I was seated next to Cliff Morgan of the BBC, an outstanding raconteur, who kept everyone amused. He would be just the sort of guest for our Professional Footballers' Association dinner.

Thursday 19 May. My social life continued when I went with Gordon Taylor, secretary of the PFA, to the Football Writers Dinner at the Café Royal. It was good to go to another dinner so that we could compare it with our own but we, and everyone else, were completely thrown when a surprise guest of honour was announced – Pelé. The great Brazilian star came across well and everyone was delighted that he had come. He presented the award to Liverpool's Kenny Dalglish.

Friday 20 May. My next engagement was the *Sunday People* awards. For the second evening in succession I was in the same company as Ron Atkinson who presented an award to another 'surprise guest' – Scottish International Charlie Nicholas. Lennie Bennett was the comedian but I didn't think he went down as well as Bob Monkhouse had 12 months earlier. I was told later that a rather 'happy' Gordon Taylor had been heard regaling the experienced Lennie Bennett as to how and why he had lost his audience.

Saturday 21 May. As if it was not bad enough missing a Cup Final the day was ruined when we were told that those not playing could not travel with the team to Wembley. We were to travel in taxis that would follow behind. Remi Moses was so upset that he even threatened going home. I went with my old university friend, Bas Barwick, so that I could watch the match from the BBC gantry. Lawrie McMenemy and Bobby Charlton were up there to discuss the respective merits of Manchester and their under-dog opponents, Brighton and Hove Albion. Bobby was highly critical of square passing as typified by Ray Wilkins and I was especially delighted when my room-mate scored what I hoped would be the winning goal.

However, it wasn't to be. Gary Stevens equalised and the draw was almost an anti-climax, albeit a welcome one after Gordon Smith missed a glorious chance for the Second Division club in the last minutes. The banquet went ahead and a handful of players went out on the town. It was all a bit of a damp squib.

Sunday 22 May. The civic reception was even more disappointing and to compound matters, the weather was awful and typical Manchester for our ride in the open-topped bus.

Monday 23 May. Plans are under way for the replay and we are going to stay in the rather plush and pleasant surroundings of the Compleat Angler on the Thames at Marlow. This time only 16 players are making the trip, which is better than the 21 which everyone felt was uncomfortably large. Hypocritically I was thankful and the fact that it has ruined my intended timetable to travel to Brazil for Channel

Four television is unimportant in the circumstances. I appreciate Atkinson's efforts to make me feel a part of things.

Thursday 26 May. Everything has gone really well over the last few days and it was reflected in the fabulous four-goal win over Brighton in the replay as Bryan Robson scored twice to add to goals from an Arnold Muhren penalty and from Norman Whiteside. I even managed to scramble into a lap of honour but I did not feel part of it. The other lads were soon off to catch the train home and I was left to reflect that the Cup Finals have been mental torture. I was really pleased for the lads, particularly the youngsters like Mike Duxbury and Alan Davies, but the realisation hit me that I should have been a part of it.

Friday 27 May. I snapped out of my depression as I caught the 22.00 flight from Heathrow to Rio. I was genuinely excited as I never thought I would get the opportunity to return and was looking forward to seeing the statue of Christ on the Corcovada, Sugar Loaf Mountain and, of course, the Brazilian Cup Final in the awesome Maracana Stadium.

Saturday 28 May. The flight was no hardship at all as I travelled business class which, though a lot more expensive than tourist, made all the difference as I could stretch out my leg. I arrived in Rio to be met by Derek Brandon who took me for a delicious fruit breakfast before we set off for the beaches of Ipanema and Copocabana in search of the traditional game of sand football so that we could do a little filming. We found only one and our Portuguese film crew interrupted the kids to introduce me and to explain what we wanted to do. They were singularly unimpressed at the prospect of having an English International footballer join in their game and my ego was done no good at all by the fact that they showed it quite openly and gave me the odd kick to encourage me to get the intrusion over with.

We finished that bit of filming and were then amazed to find the Brazilian star Adilio coaching and joining in a kick-about on the next pitch despite the fact that he was going to play for Flamengo in the Cup Final 24 hours later. It turned out that he comes from a very poor background and believes that it is his duty to encourage the youngsters all he can. I don't think that players in the English Cup Final, me included, would feel the same pang of conscience the day before the final. As the weather was so good we were all in swimming trunks and I felt slightly self conscious at being filmed next to Adilio's athletic body.

1 June – 28 August. The days have drifted into weeks and the weeks into months as I have tried to push the future to the back of my mind and concentrate on the present. At least there has been plenty to occupy me having flown straight from the magic of Rio to the unusual venue of Swaziland where Manchester United and Tottenham Hotspur were playing a series of games. I gave up any idea of training and, instead, played golf four days on the trot. It put a terrific strain on the injured leg and I was forced to develop a new stance and swing.

I returned home and finally paid some attention to my wife Jane and we set off for the States on a holiday. It wasn't fair on Jane but, without the buzz of a lot of people around me, I felt depressed as the feeling grew that there is no way I will ever play again. The more I thought of this the more I wanted to play. I wanted to share Jane's enjoyment of the holiday with her but couldn't knowing that I was getting ever closer to going back to something I didn't want to face up to.

My birthday, 9 July, has always been a day for reflection in my life, a time when I have looked back over my achievement of the year before and areas in which I could improve during the coming year. I looked back on a year of affliction and disappointment and all I could see to look forward to was playing a couple of games and then struggling, playing a couple more and then struggling again and so on. Where, I asked myself, would I be in a year's time – would I be in football at all? On that day I knew that my playing career was over but like an alcoholic I kept telling myself 'just one more'.

Bank Holiday Monday 29 August. The season started today without me but I am still training hard and hoping for a miracle and that first game of the season. I woke up not really in the mood for any kind of strenuous activity. I kept telling myself that Champions train when everyone else stops and so pushed myself to an 8 a.m. run on the local golf course. The damp, unpleasant morning reflected my own mood and I found it difficult to get going. Was it the weather which was causing the stiffness or was my knee still getting worse? I finished the run at a dispirited crawl and then got ready for the meal before the game against Nottingham Forest at Old Trafford. It was identical to the game against Queen's Park Rangers on Saturday except that the luck was with Forest this time and they won 2–1 to give us our first home defeat for 18 months.

Tuesday 30 August. My suspicions of yesterday were confirmed when I woke up to find my leg swollen and sore. Jim McGregor was amazed and could not understand why it had happened. I suggested that it had either been through running on hard ground or that my weights routine was too intensive. It provoked a heart-to-heart with Jim and we both voiced our doubts whether the leg would ever be strong enough for the type of football I wanted to play. One of my problems is that I cannot distinguish between the pain you train through and the pain by which nature warns you that you are doing yourself permanent damage. We both agreed that if I did play on for two years the damage I could do might be irreparable. We *almost* reached the decision that I should retire.

Jim made arrangements for us to see Noble the next day and even though I have been subconsciously prepared for this for a long time I returned home and was inconsolable. Conversation with Jane was impossible. I withdrew into myself and resolved to try new areas – reading, wine, food, business, everything and anything.

Wednesday 31 August. The whole day was spent in hospitals. I had arranged to visit a youngster called Jonathan Owens in St Mary's. He was recovering from a car crash and had just come out of a coma but was making good progress. When I arrived for my appointment with Noble he asked me if I would talk to a young girl whom he had operated on the day before. She had broken her leg nine months earlier, it had become infected and this was her eighth operation. She was a United fan and I tried to cheer her up with a card and some chocolates.

When we left her bedside I wondered if Noble had had an ulterior motive in taking me to see someone much worse off than me but maybe I am just becoming a little sensitive. This was my third visit to him this summer and he said how pleased he was with my progress. He insisted that the general trend has been upward despite the minor set-backs. He also told me that if there was no dramatic progress by Christmas he would operate again with an orthopaedic surgeon by his side to help assess the damage. He also referred me to a rheumatologist called Professor Jayston. He said he may be able to help me but, then again, it may be a waste of time. Christmas seemed an awful long way off but on a completely mercenary level it meant that I should qualify for a new car from the club. I would rather have a new knee.

Thursday 1 September. I visited the rheumatologist and he explained that Noble thought my reactions were far in excess of my mechanical disability and he was hoping to find out why they were. After reading my case history and examining my leg, he prescribed a drug that I had not tried before and sent me for a blood test. I was loath to start taking drugs but as they were supposed to protect the cartilage I decided to give them a try. Jayston could not find any obvious reasons for my reactions and said he would see me again when he had received the results of the blood test.

Friday 2 September. A quiet day. I had my blood test and limited my physical activity to a swim. Once again it was wait and see.

Sunday 4 September. I walked around all day with leg weights apart from a period spent doing 110 lengths in the swimming pool. Ready to try more.

Monday 5 September. Saw Jim McGregor and he was quite heartened by my exercise and told me to do half of what I was doing before the reaction. Who knew what that was, so I sat down and worked out a completely new fitness session.

110 lengths in the swimming pool plus 200 hops in the shallow end
10 pence worth of very light squash hitting
extensive yoga exercises
2 × 15-minute periods of cycling
250 step-ups, side leg raises plus straight legs and leg extensions

The squash is a new addition but it will be a good one if I increase it gradually. I have until Christmas and I must make full use of that time.

Tuesday 6 September. Typical of my impatience I put aside the slow build-up and really worked hard with three sessions well in excess of my planned programme which was a hard one even if I was fully fit. There is something inside me that drives me to do more and more once I have started. It is a kind of desperation and I forget that once I get involved the pain lessens and it is only afterwards that I pay the full price.

Wednesday 7 September. Jim was late after the Arsenal game last night so I began the warm-up on my own. When he arrived he was impressed by my 'Zico' legs! The joint felt good but somehow different, to any feeling I had felt before. I had a two-hour session of 't'ai chi' in the afternoon but I was not happy about standing for that length of time and I promptly wrote to the teacher giving some excuse for finishing my lessons. I could think of more profitable ways of spending my time. I felt drained after the full session the day before and curtailed my efforts at the health club but still managed 110 lengths in the pool. There was no swelling but it still didn't feel right.

Thursday 8 September. My leg felt and looked 'podgy' but when I tested it I found I still had full range of movement and there was no reason why I should not carry on with the work. In the afternoon I headed for the PFA offices and while I was there I received a telephone call from Derek Potter of the *Daily Express* who told me that he knew how difficult I was finding it to recover and that he was wrestling with his conscience as to whether or not to break the story that I was finished. I don't think he will use the story but I decided to try and avoid the Press for the moment. Far more helpful was my chat with Gordon Taylor who said that the best policy was to do everything that the club told me and to take it from there.

Friday 9 September. My faith was misplaced. I received a very early telephone call from Peter Fitton of the *Sun* to tell me that Derek Potter and Bob Russell of the *Daily Mirror* had both broken the story that I was to retire. At least Peter had spoken to me which was more than Russell had done. I suspect that he was Potter's source. They know more than I do for though the knee is puffy, it is not very tender and I can still move it fully.

Saturday 10 September. I had some limited sessions before and after the game against Luton Town. Watching these games is still very strange to me. For 70 or 80 minutes I was not bothered at all, just fully engrossed with the events on the pitch. But for 10 or 20 minutes I found myself thinking that this could not be me sitting in the stand instead of playing. How could it be when I had gone four seasons without missing a match. I had been going to break all appearance records. I had been going to play until I was 40. I had been going to be in the England side more times than Stanley Matthews or Tom Finney. How could something as seemingly minor as this knee injury stop me. However, it can and I had to wear a thick bandage when Jane and I went to Rookery Hall to celebrate a friend's birthday.

Sunday 11 September. We had friends coming to lunch so I went through all my routines by mid-morning including three sessions on the bike and all my weights.

Monday 12 September. I went to see Jim hoping to start running. That turned out to be the height of optimism as Jim was confused by the state of my leg. If it can't stand the strain I have put on it then I have problems. Jim told me to forget about training and to go on holiday, anything at all that would occupy my mind until Noble returns from his holiday.

All sorts of thoughts filled my head. Had I had the best treatment? Being hypercritical I didn't think so but then again I am not knowledge-able enough to judge. I have always consciously tried to avoid swearing but it was the only way I could relieve my pent-up frustrations and I ran through my entire repertoire a dozen times on the way home in the car.

Tuesday 13 September. I had time on my hands; time to think and to speculate. Would any other future hold the same thrills, highs, lows that football has given me. Roll on Monday.

Wednesday 14 September. To hell with it. What did I have to lose. I woke up wanting to train and that is what I did. Just working myself into a sweat made me feel better. There were further distractions later in the day as I sat on a Football League tribunal to discuss the sacking of Manchester City winger Peter Bodak and to assess the disputed transfer value of Steve Whitton, who had moved from Coventry City to West Ham United. We supported the player upsetting Manchester City while Coventry's poor presentation of their case, having sent only their assistant secretary, meant that West Ham, with manager John Lyall, secretary and two directors present, won their case.

Thursday 15 September. I woke up to discover that the swelling around the joint had gone down and immediately decided to go for a 45-minute run – I lasted exactly 5 minutes and limped back home. As a result I went to a Tranmere Rovers' dinner as guest speaker and made a very ordinary speech. If they had known what was on my mind I am sure they would have understood.

Sunday 18 September. The monthly PFA meeting at the Grand Hotel in Manchester helped break the monotony since I have conquered my desperate urge to train.

Thursday 20 September. It was almost as if I was standing on the outside looking in on my own life especially when my next-door-neighbour Bob Carol-Gees asked me to appear on a television programme called *Hold Tight* with Spit the Dog. Bob explained that the programme was being filmed for screening in a month's time and that the interview would be about my returning to the team after such a long absence. I couldn't tell them I was on the verge of retiring but I didn't feel too bad about it as they asked me as a last minute stand-in only.

Wednesday 21 September. At last Noble was back from his holiday and I arrived early for my appointment. The decision was for an immediate operation. There is no alternative and it came as no surprise. In fact I was relieved that something positive was being done after biding time for so long.

Friday 30 September. The days have shot by. Time has been filled in with a presentation to Franny Lee; PFA work; watching squash at Warrington; a sportsman's dinner at Rochdale and meetings with an agent. But at last the day of the operation has arrived. No one needed to tell me that this was make or break. I sensed it. My friend and accountant Mike Prescott picked me up after breakfast to take me to the BUPA Hospital in Manchester. I went through the familiar pre-op checks and routines before going down to the operating theatre at tea-time to play my usual game with the anaesthetist of seeing if I could stay awake for longer than my usual count of three which I couldn't.

It must have been two or three hours later when I came round and the first thing I did was to feel gingerly down the bed for the size of bandage, normally a good pointer to the seriousness of the operation. This time it told me nothing – or maybe I didn't want to know. A nurse brought me a glass of water and was followed in by Noble. 'Good or bad news!' I asked. He signalled that I should wait until the nurse had left the room but I knew from his face what the answer was. The tears welled up with emotion and frustration of the past few months and the dam burst when he said gently: 'I am afraid I am going to have to advise you to retire.'

My world fell in on top of me.

3

Dear Steve

Grown men don't cry, particularly if they are professional footballers who play for Manchester United and England. However, I did when the realisation hit me that I was no longer a professional footballer. Jonathan Noble was a great help to me that day and he sat with me for five minutes, ten minutes I don't know how long. Why, I kept thinking, should it happen to me when there was still so much that I wanted to do in the game? Gradually I became aware that Noble was trying to ask me questions. Did I want to stay in hospital for the night? All I wanted to do was to get away and I managed to get through on the telephone between sobs to my wife Jane.

They wheeled me through the hospital and I felt everyone watching me with a sympathy I did not want. I wanted to hurt myself, do something violent but all I did was whimper. Jane picked me up and all the way home I did not say a word. I slumped down in a chair and stopped crying only long enough to answer a couple of telephone calls. Inevitably the first was from Jim McGregor who had just heard the news. As my parents were still on holiday I asked him if the announcement from the club could wait until the next day after I had had a chance to tell them when they returned home.

The following call was from Ray Wilkins. I appreciated it even though he refused to believe that the specialist was right. I would, he insisted, soon be back. 'No Ray I won't,' I replied. Jane sat with me for a long while until my silence finally drove her to bed. I sat sightlessly watching a video on the television until pangs of hunger aroused me. The fridge could only yield a packet of deeply frozen chocolate eclairs and a few cans of lager. At that moment it was almost like a final breaking, once and for all, with training. I ate and drank and finally went to bed, eyes wide open and thoughts a long way from Delamere Forest.

Things did not improve much the following day when I turned on the television to hear Ian St John announcing my retirement. I wouldn't be able to break the news to my parents myself after all and I sank into a deep depression, very much as I had when my grandfather died. The one image that I couldn't get out of my mind was that bit of grass I thought of as my own at Old Trafford.

The Sunday papers heralded another bad morning. I went through the comments from manager Ron Atkinson after the 3–3 draw with Norwich while Jim McGregor was quoted as saying: 'The bone is flaking and there is nothing anyone can do about it. He will have to nurse the knee through the rest of his life. To continue top-level football would have done irreparable harm.' Coming from Jim it just made everything irrevocable.

Tommy Docherty, the man who took me to Manchester United, wrote in the *Sunday People*: 'You get twopenny players, villains and then the like of Steve Coppell. He is absolutely irreplaceable and a smashing lad. What a tragedy. I'm sad because at 28 he should just be coming into his prime. It's a great blow at a time when England is struggling. It's also a jolt for United and the lad himself. He has played on through his injury for a couple of years putting the club before himself. That's typical.

'If he had thought a little more of himself things might have been different but that's not Stevie's style. He is a clever boy and British football should do all it can to make sure they make the most of his brains and his ability. Surely if he wants it – there must be a career for him in the Football League or the Football Association. He can still be a very big name in the game.'

I then read some news of a different nature which made me feel very humble and selfish. Bob Kerry, the Education Officer and my colleague at the Professional Footballers' Association, had died of a heart attack on a fun run. It acted like a cold shower and suddenly everything was put into perspective. Here I was, 28 years old and in comparatively good health. Bob was 42 and married with 4 children. When he died he had been raising money for charity.

From then on I read the tributes and my mail in a different light. I was extremely gratified when my former England boss, Ron Greenwood, telephoned to offer to bring an England team to Old Trafford for a testimonial while the current England manager, Bobby Robson, told

Daily Telegraph reporter Colin Gibson: 'It is a heavy blow and a sad loss not only for Manchester United and England but for the game in general. He was a player and a person of the highest calibre. He was a great crosser of the ball, a great goalscorer and a remarkable worker. When I took over the England job he was one of the two World Class players I was looking to build the side around.'

The following are just a small selection of the letters I received from people in all walks of life. I haven't reproduced them here for self glorification but to say some kind of thank you to everyone concerned and to show that football is not about backstabbing, birds, booze and 'me' articles. Somewhere very near the surface the great majority of footballers, managers and referees care about the game and the people in it.

* * *

Joe Gallagher, Billy Rodaway and I were team-mates in the first Liverpool Primary XI (Under 12) back in the 1965–66 season and though we were never particularly close, we have always followed one another's careers as this letter from Joe Gallagher amply illustrates. It was one of the most touching and most appreciated that I received.

> Joe Gallagher
> Sparrow Hawk Hotel
> Burnley, Lancs
> 3 October 1983

Dear Steve,

Out of every footballer in the country there were only always two players I wanted to do really well, Steve Coppell and Billy Rodaway, for reasons I won't go into and which you already know.

Steve, when I heard the news I was absolutely choked, as I'm sure millions of football supporters were, but believe me I felt it deep down in my guts. Everyone, including your team-mates, will offer sympathy and like the fantastic 'pro' and lad you are you will put on a brave face and say 'thank you' but deep down your heart will be crying and saying, 'why does it have to be me they are talking to'.

My family may not pass on their feelings about all this but I would like you to know they take all this as a personal tragedy and my Dad more than anyone. He would always say when he watched us play at Penny Lane, Kirby, or anywhere else, that that little No. 7 would one day play for England. At the time we didn't take much notice because we didn't really understand, a year or so later I started to understand what playing for England meant and I thought the same only I envisaged that Billy Rodaway would be with you in the same team – the only man to answer why he didn't do as well as us is Billy himself. Enough of the past, I don't want to sound boring, I'm sure you will get a million letters saying the same old repetitive things.

I know how I feel but I cannot put it on paper. I hope you try and hold your head up and show everybody that the determined Steve Coppell of the past is not going to go under like a lot of people would if they had suffered a disappointment like this. You are big enough in mind if not in strength to go on in life and make a bigger name than you did when you were playing. I really hope so.

Don't forget your Mum and Dad will be more upset than you, Steve, so you must be strong and look after them in these difficult times.

I know Manchester United will look after you as much as possible, but if I can help in anyway at all you only have to ask. Go on and show the country what a clever little bugger you are and that you don't need a pair of football boots to earn a living. I will be rooting for you every day Steve and pray that you do well in life. I'm sure you will.

GOD BLESS YOU STEVE

> Best wishes,
> *Joe Gallagher*

Through playing international football, club rivals can also be team-mates and I became particularly friendly with Liverpool's consistent defender Phil Neal. I enjoyed playing against and with him and I always felt that our styles complemented each other in the England team.

Phil Neal
Formby
Merseyside
4 October 1983

Dear Steve,

I can imagine how you must be feeling right now. Nevertheless, after talking to you just the other week I felt I had to put pen to paper and to say how shocked I was to hear the news. Not only will you be badly missed in the game but I was looking forward to your return to the national side where you sparked off confidence and inspiration to those around you.

However, with your experience, knowledge and ambassadorial qualities I'm sure you will be successful whatever you eventually decide to do.

Steve, if there is anything I can do please do not hesitate to call me at home anytime.

Best wishes,
Phil Neal

The nice thing about my mailbag from my fellow professionals was that not all of the writers knew me particularly well. I had met Martin Dobson only once or twice and his letter is further evidence of the ties that exist between players.

Martin Dobson
Burnley FC
1 October 1983

Dear Steve,

I've just read that you've had to retire because of the seriousness of your knee injury. For me it's a very sad day. Your behaviour both on and off the field has been exemplary and I can't help wondering why these disasters happen to all the best people. I suppose it's because they have the qualities to overcome any set backs. I just hope that this applies to you and that whatever you decide to do in the future is a tremendous success. The old football clichés keep coming through at this time: 'Keep battling' and 'don't let the bastards grind you down'. I remember when I got a 'free' at 18 from Bolton. A very good friend whose opinion I respected a lot told me, 'perhaps it's for the best in the long term'. It turned out to be true but it seemed somewhat condescending at the time. Let's hope this is the same with you.

All the best.

Regards,
Martin Dobson

Not just footballers, either, the next letter was from John Goggins, the secretary of the Referees' Association.

John Goggins
Association of Football League
Referees and Linesmen
5 October 1983

Dear Steve,
   The manner in which news of your enforced retirement from your playing career has been received is truly indicative of the respect in which you are held in the game. On behalf of all the members of the association I join with the many others who chorus their tribute to a fine, exemplary professional footballer and express their sorrow at the news. We hope and pray for you to have the courage to bear what must be great personal sadness for you and your family; a sadness which will be overcome by the same kind of professional approach which you have always shown.

   It is to be hoped also that your natural gift of high intelligence allied to the level of knowledge and experience in the game will not be lost and that you will soon find a niche where you can give evidence of these skills for everyone's benefit.

   May I add my own sorrow and good wishes for your future happiness and welfare.

Sincerely,
John Goggins

Everyone at Manchester United, of course, was sympathetic, even those on the periphery of the club. The following letter was from Tommy Docherty's wife.

Agnes Docherty
Hale
Altrincham
1 October 1983

Dear Steve,

I send my regrets, with many others, that your active soccer career is over.

I sympathise with the pain you have suffered – my eldest son, Michael, had to undergo three operations on his left knee prior to compulsory retirement from the game and I was a witness to the heartache involved.

You gave a great measure of joy to followers of United and England – you have wonderful memories to cherish – all on video, so fortunate for the players of the game today.

I know you will have the good sense to be thankful for the good years in football – I am glad you have the 'grey matter' to start a new career Steve.

Go to it!

Sincere best wishes,
Agnes Docherty

Tranmere Rovers, my only other professional club, were also quick to respond to the news with the then secretary Jack Butterfield and the supporters' club secretary, neither of whom I knew particularly well, sending their best wishes.

Jack Butterfield
Tranmere Rovers RC
8 October 1983

Dear Steve,

On behalf of everyone at Tranmere Rovers I wish to say how downhearted we all are at the tragic news last weekend. There were rumours – at least we had hoped that they were only rumours – about your injury problem but it still came as a great shock. As a person who went out of the game myself through injury, I believe I know the feeling – it is, very simply, awful!

I can only say that we all wish you well in whatever you decide to do in the future. If there is any way we can help – however small the action – we will try our best. If a full testimonial (I mean other than just a game) is granted, please let me know and we will arrange a sportsman's evening at Prenton Park.

Best wishes to you and your family,
Jack Butterfield

I had spent a great deal of time in the care of the England medical staff, so it was particularly good to hear from them. Vernon Edwards, the team doctor, was always a friendly 'ear', not only to me but to all the players.

Dr V. A. Edwards
Watford, Herts
3 October 1983

Dear Steve,

I was very saddened, on my return from holiday yesterday, to hear the news that you have been forced to retire on medical grounds.

Of course I cannot really comment on your decision as I do not know the full findings on your knee joint, but as a doctor I do feel that you are very wise if there was evidence of degenerative changes in the knee. Having said this, of course the game is going to suffer considerably with you no longer gracing the field with your skills and determination.

I hope very much that you will be able to carry on as chairman of the PFA as I believe that body desperately needs somebody with your insight to guide it.

I hope very much that we might meet up in some future time, but in the meantime, my best wishes to you and your family.

Kind regards.

Yours sincerely,
Vernon Edwards

Considering that one specialist who had treated me on a couple of occasions, Sidney Rose, is a director of Manchester City Football Club he looked after me pretty well.

Sidney Rose
West Didsbury
Manchester
26 October 1983

Dear Steve,
It was with great sadness that I heard you had to retire from the game, not only because of our personal relationship, but because of the vast amount of pleasure that you have given not only to me but to everyone who has seen you play.

If your example was followed both on and off the field by most of our footballers, the football grounds up and down the country would be much happier places to be.

I would like to wish you every success in whatever new venture you undertake.

Yours,
Sidney Rose

But it was not only close friends and acquaintances from my past who wrote to me but also people whom I'd never met. One thing that my daily post showed me was what a universal game football truly is. The sport, through television and the Press in particular, reaches everywhere – to people and to places abroad that you would think hadn't even heard of Manchester United or its footballers. Many wrote to me direct and others to the club or to Brian Moore of London Weekend Television whose programme and match commentaries are seen and heard world-wide.

Sister Jane Anne CP
4 October 1983

Dear Steve,

No doubt you have had many many letters since you announced your retirement but probably not too many from nuns. Yes, I am a nun, an American who has lived in this country for 16 years. In that time I have grown to love the game of soccer. I come from a city in Kentucky, but only minutes from Cincinnati, Ohio so I have been an avid sports fan for much of my 60 years! My Superior and I share an intense interest in sports. Neither of us has ever been to a soccer game but we have seldom missed *Match of the Day*, *Sports Night* or what have you.

We will continue to watch these games but oh my, how we will miss you in Manchester United's team – but especially England. You have given us so much enjoyment in watching you play the game with your heart in every match and your skills that truly have no 'match'. We will really miss you.

I have two very young nephews, eight and ten years old, who play the game quite well for their age. My hope is that they will someday play the game as you have, though they have never had the chance to see you play. I'm certain you have been a great inspiration to many a young footballer.

My Superior joins me in wishing you all the best in the coming years. We are grateful to have been able to see such a great lad as you play the game with such skill and determination.

Be assured of our prayers in all that you do.

Sincerely,
Sister Jane Anne

Father John Williamson
St Teresa's Carmelite Priory
Gregory Terrace
Brisbane
Australia
18 October 1983

Dear Steve,

I was very sorry to see the sad news today in the Press concerning your knee injury. I want to express my sympathy to you and your family and wish you every blessing in your future.

I've only ever seen you on TV, both playing and interviews and read about you in papers and soccer magazines – yet your talent and dedication to soccer have given me and millions of others a lot of great entertainment – for this Steve, sincere gratitude for who you are, and the speed and precision of your play – which for consistency ranks you among the great post-war stars. You come over in the media as a modest and unpretentious man who has shown great loyalty to club and country – it's not just about chasing a ball around, it's character and personality and certainly I hope you will remain in the public arena where your personality has still got everything to offer the youth by way of example.

I will keep you and your family in my prayers and ask God to be with you in your disappointment and sustain you in your courage. God bless you Steve,

John Williamson

There were others, many, many others. Sympathy, advice, good wishes, offers of jobs. As I answered them I felt more and more humbled that so many people had taken the trouble to write to the lad from the back streets of Liverpool. How does that saying go? Better to have loved and lost than never to have loved at all. Certainly football had opened up a great many doors and taken me to a great many places around the world I probably would not have seen otherwise.

Football had given me up – but was there any reason why I should give up football? Maybe there was a club and a chairman somewhere who would be prepared to make me the youngest manager in the Football League.

4

Schooldays

One could not say professional football originally beckoned as a career in my youth. Of course, like any other soccer-daft Liverpudlian, there was nothing I wanted more, but unfortunately I didn't top five feet until I was aged 17. There was no string of schoolboy honours and no scouts knocking on the door of our terrace house. Both Liverpool and Everton took fright at my size and even a lunatic magpie earned more column inches in the local papers from its football exploits than I did.

This particular creature hardly helped shape my football career but he certainly ensured that my only interest in birds of the feathered variety is to have them plucked, cooked and served on a plate. The bird was famous in Liverpool, earning features in the local Liverpool daily papers, the *Post* and the *Echo*, for its exploits at Quarry Bank School. Its name was Monty and its speciality was attacking any young footballer that took its fancy. It was a crazy bird, but a sly one. It would even make dummy runs to fool its prey, swooping down on some unsuspecting lad and pecking the back of his neck. It forced one 14-year-old goalkeeper into premature retirement; the lad simply refused to play because the bird would sit on his crossbar, attacking him at the most inconvenient moments.

I used to watch all this with some contempt, never being able to understand why the victim didn't hit the scrawny thing or grab it by the wing. I found out why when I suddenly became its next target. It must have been my gold-coloured football shirt which caught its attention for, before I knew it, it began dive-bombing me like a World War II aeroplane. The bird was too quick and smart to hit or catch and it was impossible to play a casual through ball with Monty pecking at your head. It soon had me racing for the shelter of the dressing rooms and even followed me there; when I hung my shirt at the window it began battering the glass. In the end they had to call in the RSPCA to take it away before it did someone some real harm. I certainly thought

Alfred Hitchcock's film *The Birds* realistic when I went to see it at the local Odeon and my mother swears that when we walked by the town hall and the pigeons took off, I would duck. I still do when there are birds about – and Trafalgar Square is a nightmare.

Football frightened me far less and despite my size I was always ready to join in a kick-about as far back as I can remember. It was a way of life round the back streets of Liverpool in those days and far more popular than hanging around on street corners as they do today. I was born in Liverpool's Walton Hospital on 9 July 1955, the second son of three children born to Jim and Ena Coppell. My brother, Kevin, is five and a half years older than me and my sister, Christine, is two and half years younger.

My first home was a ground-floor flat in a ten-storey block called Coronation Court (no prizes for guessing it was built in 1953) in a tough neighbourhood called Sparrow Hall, an overspill area on the outskirts of Liverpool. You had only to step outside our front door to walk straight into a game of street football, often 20 strong per side with one road pitched against the other. My brother Kevin was always taking part in these and by the time I reached four or five I was getting the odd game, stuck between the coats as goalkeeper or making up the numbers with my brother acting as my minder. Whatever happened to those street games? When I walk through Liverpool, London or Manchester these days, I don't see any games of football at all.

All my early memories are centred on soccer which, along with pop music, dominated Liverpool in my formative years. I remember my disappointment when the music master at Ranworth Square County Primary School tapped me on the shoulder and told me I would never make the school choir! I was also told, of course, that I would never be a footballer. They were not only wrong about the football bit but also about the music for I was eventually involved in three top thirty hits! However, I have to admit that I was only part of an 'assisted' choir and I recorded songs twice with Manchester United before Cup Finals and once with England before going to the World Cup Finals in Spain. I also helped make an album with United consisting of such memorable tracks as: 'Does Your Chewing Gum Lose Its Flavour on the Goalpost Overnight'; 'Onward Sexton Soldiers'; 'United We Stand' and 'Red Sails in the Sunset'. But it owed more to modern electronic wizardry than the Coppell vocal chords and while Elton John might take six months to make an LP on location in the Caribbean, ours took a couple of hours one afternoon in a converted warehouse in Manchester.

It was probably in those early street games and the occasional away game in West Derby Cemetery in Norris Green (nicknamed Wembley because of the lush grass) that I perfected my lethal finishing ability from two yards. My age and size meant that if I wasn't put in goal, because no one else wanted to play there, I would be a 'goal hanger'.

It was a tough existence. If your street had the best fighters you usually had the best team but it never went as far as gang warfare because the underdog would usually run away to fight another day and the police were rarely needed to clean things up. In those days the leader was usually the biggest lad but it did not always mean that he was the best player.

My first organised football was at my primary school when, in my very first year, a teacher named Miss Lydiate divided us into teams. She must have been fairly perceptive for when I told her I didn't know which position I preferred she put me out on the right wing. School was good in those days. Between the ages of seven and eleven, the difference in height, shape and weight was not so pronounced and by the time I reached third year, a lad named Steven Whitaker and I were running the team and playing where we wanted. With some success, too, I might add for we won leagues and a couple of cups. The academic side wasn't bad either and I was lucky enough to be made head boy.

My guiding lights in those days were the games master Owen Griffiths (I still call him Mr Griffiths) and the headmaster David McKay. Both were prepared to give up a great deal of their spare time with Mr Griffiths, who arrived in our second year, encouraging us to play with a tennis ball in the school playground during our break time, saying that that was how Stanley Matthews and Tom Finney had learned their skills. He also used to give up his lunch hour to kick a ball around with us.

Mr McKay took me to Goodison Park and Anfield. I gazed in awe at the photographs of the great Everton teams around Goodison but with disappointment at the sign forbidding us to go onto the pitch itself because undersoil heating had just been installed. I tried in vain to spot a famous face but there were no players around. Anfield, the home of

Liverpool FC, was even more exciting because they were my team. I had started watching them in the 1959–60 season, going along with my Dad and my brother who would leave me to my own devices in the boys' pen while they stood on the Kop.

I recall only too well that first great Bill Shankly side with: Lawrence; Moran; Byrne; Yates; Smith; Stephenson; Callaghan; St John; Hunt; Milne; and Thompson – especially Peter Thompson. I had a soft spot for him because he was a winger but I also admired Ian St John and Rowdy Yates while Shanks was my idol. Ronnie Moran, such a key backroom figure with Liverpool during their great years, also stands out because whenever we hung around waiting for autographs he would not only sign them but also make the effort to stay and chat for five or ten minutes, asking what school we went to and what positions we played in.

That boys' pen at Anfield was a little kingdom all of its own. It was the older lads who sneaked in and ran the place, dictating who stood where, while abusing and spitting at the unfortunate adults who made the mistake of standing too close to our fence. Around the end of October and beginning of November, fireworks replaced the spitting and deeper into the winter it was icy snowballs. They were right little tearaways and, being small, I tried to keep well out of the way and if they spotted me and demanded my can of Coke or Mars bar, under threat of a kicking, I gave in gracefully.

However, it was what happened in front of me that really captured my imagination; this was when the seeds were first sown of pulling on a red shirt and playing professional football for Liverpool. I was hooked. I even went to some of the Central League reserve games, running onto the pitch on one famous occasion and pinching a clod of the sodden turf to take home and cultivate in the back garden. By the time we had walked home, however, it had disintegrated and run through our fingers. I was even brave enough to stand with the swaying, singing, scarf-waving comedians on the Kop. I only stood there three times because everyone was so closely huddled together that if someone wanted a pee they would roll up the 'Footie Echo' and do it. If you happened to be standing in front you would feel a warm, damp patch spreading on your trousers but there was nothing you could do about it.

I fancied my chances of making it in those days because of the success of my school team and the fact that I was picked for the very first Liverpool Primary XI along with players like: Billy Rodaway, who went on to play for Burnley, Peterborough, Blackpool and now ironically with Tranmere; Joe Gallagher, who made his name with Birmingham City before moving on to Wolves, West Ham, Burnley and Halifax; and John Highams who was an apprentice at Liverpool. Now that is not a bad record at all for 11-year-olds, especially as our football was confined to friendlies against teams from Manchester, Elsmere Port and other local areas. Nowadays the scouts would be watching such a successful little team but then we were considered too young and I waited in vain for an approach.

I was also concentrating on my schoolwork and while I longed to play professional football I also desperately wanted to pass the Eleven-plus. Dad was one of a family of eight and Mum one of six and none of them had managed to get into grammar school. I wanted to be the first and although I was consistently in the top 10 out of 90-odd children, I still did extra homework for Mr Griffiths to ensure my pass. It was a big day when I heard that I had passed my Eleven-plus. Football, however, even played a part in my choice of school. The headmaster, Mr McKay, wanted me to go to Quarry Bank because even though it was on the other side of the city, it was the route that a certain Joe Royle had taken. Mr McKay was always talking about Joe and holding him up as an example for me to follow. I was quite happy to take Mr McKay's advice and Joe, who had starred for Everton, Manchester City and England before turning to management, obviously thought as highly of him because we both visited Mr McKay in hospital shortly before he died.

Mr McKay was a lovely warm person who created a marvellous atmosphere in the school. He made school life interesting and different. He would give you a penny if you took a catch at cricket and he introduced a prize called a 'thumb-nail clap' for anyone who did well at football when the whole school applauded you at assembly. The school motto was 'Brave and Calm' which fitted the headmaster like a glove. Even though I worked hard at my lessons I still found time to play cricket (I batted and kept wicket) and run the 100 yards for the school.

Quarry Bank Grammar School was different again, and the motto this time was Latin, 'Ex Hoc Metallo Virtutem', meaning 'Out of this Quarry comes Virtue'. It was a posh school in a nice area that drew boys from good homes. I will always remember a lesson in technical drawing when we were asked to do a plan of the street where we lived. There they were, the semis and the detached houses in private roads and cul-de-sacs. At the time I lived in an end terrace but drew it so that it came out as a semi. It wasn't so much being snobbish as not wanting to be singled out and to be thought of as poor or different. A year later the school became comprehensive but, happily, in name only for it was still basically the same staff teaching the same pupils.

The standard of teaching was high and my work continued to progress quite satisfactorily, which was more than I could say about my football. Suddenly my height became important. I seemed to have stopped growing altogether and remained under five feet while my contemporaries were nearing six feet and more. I don't care what anyone says, in those circumstances a good, big player will always beat a good little player. It stands to reason. You may outplay him a few times but, by and large, you would still be overshadowed by the larger, more muscular boy. I was still as keen as ever on football but, it seemed, the game was no longer as keen on me. Not only did I fail to make the first team but I even struggled to keep a regular place in the second and made frequent appearances in the third team. It was hardly the springboard to a future career in the game and there were always schoolmasters willing to tell me that and emphasise how few boys made it all the way – especially when they were in the school's third team!

The one person to keep faith in my ability was my former headmaster David McKay and through his contacts he was able to arrange for me to enter Liverpool's schoolboy trials. My new headmaster, Mr Pobjoy, refused to allow me to go because Joe Royle had followed the same path and missed far too much schoolwork because of the demands of training and playing for Liverpool schoolboys. Looking back the headmaster was right and I discovered later that I wouldn't have had a chance in any case. Again it was my height which caused the problems and dashed the persistent Mr McKay's and my hopes. As I could not train during the school term, Mr McKay agreed with the Liverpool youth coach Jeff Twentyman that I should play for the 'C' team against a team of touring West German schoolboys during the Easter holiday.

Here was my chance to show them what I could do and, with my boots well dubbined and my hair neatly combed, I turned up and told them who I was. Twentyman took one look at me and another at the big German side and said something along the lines of: 'Not today thank you' and told me that the club would be in touch next season. I never received that longed-for call and, instead, found myself training with the 'enemy', Everton, again courtesy of Mr McKay who remained convinced of my potential and refused to accept defeat.

I gave it my all for four or five months but at the end of the season, at an age when they should have been offering me terms as an apprentice, I was once more told that they would be in touch. It would have been easy, years later, to have thumbed my nose at both them and Liverpool and have said, 'told you so' but the truth of the matter is that both of them were absolutely spot on. I was nowhere near good enough at that stage.

Life, in fact, was cruel for a teenager in the midst of puberty especially when you are still a boy and the rest of your year are young men. It meant taking a lot of showers on my own and taking far less interest in girls than the rest of my mates. There were 5 classes consisting of about 30 pupils each in my year at Quarry Bank and I suppose 60 or 70 of those were girls and as they reached puberty long before us boys, every one of them towered over the smallest boy in the group.

It meant that I knew little of the fumblings and gropings which went on behind the bicycle sheds and the playing pavilion. The only advantage of being a schoolboy midget was that it was the era of the mini-skirt and just because I was out of the action did not mean that I was not interested. I was always on the look-out, or should I say the look-up, for one of those extra short mini-skirts!

Having been rejected by the girls and overlooked by football I should have had all the incentive needed to concentrate on my studies but though I was reasonably bright I did little work for two or three years and, before I knew where I was, I was confronted with my 'O' levels. Now, in my opinion, the 'O' level examinations are even more important than 'A' levels because they help decide your whole future. By the time mine came around I was so certain of my capabilities that I took the precaution of having an alternative. Had I failed my 'O' levels I was all set to follow my father, Jim, into the Royal Navy as an artificer apprentice. Fortunately I never had to find out what the title meant as I scraped through six of my eight 'O' levels, albeit with horrible grades.

As I was no longer going to sea to see the world I had to decide on which subjects to take for 'A' level and I returned to Quarry Bank and went up to the sixth form ready to take economics, physics and biology. I had one look at the syllabuses, took fright and settled for English, history and economics even though English was not considered one of my better subjects. In those days I wanted to be a schoolteacher with half an eye on the physical education side. Football remained an abiding passion as I continued to watch Liverpool most weeks while moving up to a permanent place in the second team, and even making the odd appearance for the school first eleven. Nothing too spectacular, however. The big break-through came when I linked up with some of my old primary team-mates at Norris Green Boys' Club. We trained two nights a week and, at the same time, I started to grow a little taller.

The Boys' Club League was surprisingly tough and physical and I was lucky to play alongside a six foot three inch centre forward named Colin Shennan, who was not only a smashing bloke but also a very good footballer. He played his own game and still found time to take a few knocks on my behalf. The combination was a good one and we managed to reach the final of the Liverpool Boys' Club Association Cup. We lost 2–0 to Tuebrook Boys' Club but it meant that, at last, I had played on my beloved Anfield. It was almost certainly Norris Green Boys' Club and, probably Colin Shennan, that brought about such a dramatic change in my life, as we were both invited to go to Tranmere Rovers for trials. We played in a match and I scored a hat-trick. Colin had laid two of those goals on a plate for me but I was asked back and he was not. It could so easily have worked out that he would have become the professional footballer and me the school-teacher. Instead Colin is now a draughtsman in Liverpool and I still keep in touch and like to hear how he is getting on.

It just goes to show what a lottery the whole business of selection is at that age when luck as often as judgement can be the deciding factor whether or not a youngster makes the grade. I was doubly lucky for I had an alternative and though I never gave up hope of becoming a professional footballer, I knew I had to work at my studies as well.

Then everything happened at the same time, as I had both my university work and my football to pursue.

The whole affair of coaching schookids is getting too serious but professional football is such big business it is like trying to halt a runaway train. Schools of Excellence and Bobby Robson's live-in course at Lilleshall are all very well but, somehow, it seems all wrong to me that coaches should be showing 12-year-old boys how to tackle, pass, close down and play 4–2–4, even to the extent of bringing over coaches from Holland to teach them how to dribble like the stars. The greatest players were those like Johan Cruyff, Pelé, George Best and Denis Law because their skills were natural and not taught.

I believe that kids learn to play football because they want to and they do it by playing five-a-side in the street or 'three pots and in'. That is when they learn such abilities as innovation and improvisation as a plastic ball bounces off a cobblestone or awkwardly rebounds off a wall. If the present emphasis on coaching techniques continues and a class of children is taught the 'Cruyff Flip', we will finish up with an army of clones all programmed to react in the same way.

I would have had a great deal more faith in the Lilleshall concept of creaming off the best boys from around the country if it had been designed, developed and paid for by the Football Association instead of using a sponsor's money. Now I have nothing against General Motors, far from it, but it does make you wonder whether the money on offer prompted the idea rather than the other way around. In the end its success will be judged on results and it needs only one of these boys to come through the Lilleshall system for it to be acclaimed. Bobby Robson was careful to choose the best coaches and to put Dave Sexton in charge and though Bobby himself is unlikely to reap the long-term benefits for England, the clubs should certainly do so and I would anticipate as many as 15 of the students coming through and 'making' it at club level.

The project will be successful because there will be the time to work with the country's top youngsters but I am afraid the regional Schools of Excellence cannot possibly provide the same individual coaching attention and they can try only to create robots who all follow the same principles when it would probably be better to pick two sides, give them shirts, throw them a ball and let them get on with it. The old

method of signing on lads as associate schoolboys when they are 14
and then giving a lucky few apprenticeships at 16 is fading into the dim
and distant past. I remember when I first went to Tranmere I felt like
a spare part for the first four or five months and as I cleaned the
dressing rooms and swept the terraces I could not help but feel that I
was cheap labour.

The Government helped come up with the answer when they introduced the Youth Training scheme, whereby they pay youngsters a
nominal wage to learn a trade. This way they can come to clubs as
apprentice players, or on the groundstaff, work in the offices or help
with the lotteries. When Wrexham played Roma in the European Cup
Winners' Cup in the 1984 season there were 3 of these lads on the
bench including a 16-year-old goalkeeper; what an experience for them!
I have used them myself at Crystal Palace while Coventry City had a
whole team of the boys playing in a local league in the same season.

The Professional Footballers' Association have been keen for some
time to encourage young professionals to carry on with their studies
and add an extra string to their bow. The PFA will play an increasingly
important role in this respect in the coming years. It seems just common
sense to someone such as me who was forced to quit playing so early.
However, when I left Quarry Bank School for Liverpool University,
playing for Manchester United and England was not even a dream.

5

Tranmere Rovers

I almost threw away any chance of a professional football career when I turned down Tranmere Rovers chief scout Eddie Edwards' first offer of a trial! Strange, isn't it, that after yearning to play football throughout my childhood I should suddenly decide that revising for my 'A' levels, with a place at university in view, was infinitely more important. The fact was that I was working very hard at my studies and had no illusions over the possibility of a Football League side offering me my fortune, even though I had grown taller and filled out.

When Eddie Edwards came back again with the same offer a couple of weeks later, I was in the right frame of mind for a diversion, fed up with my studies and ready for a game of football, and off I went to Prenton Park with my mate Colin Shennan and my boots to score the three most critical goals of my career. They did enough to convince Tranmere that they should offer me a place at the club, on amateur terms (legitimate expenses only, honest!).

Exams were over and there was only the one nagging doubt in my mind as to whether or not I should go pre-season training with Third Division Tranmere and that was should I go on holiday with my Mum and Dad. They were off to Tenby and the offer was tempting. It was touch and go until an old hero of mine, former Liverpool goalkeeper Tommy Lawrence, offered me a daily lift to the ground along with the ex-Bolton defender Sid Farrimond. The chance to rub shoulders with two old professionals and to listen to their footballing tales seemed to be too good an opportunity to miss.

However, all through the summer weeks of training I still believed that my future lay in taking my degree at Liverpool University and maybe using my experience at Tranmere to find a nice, comfortable non-League side. (I had also applied to Leeds University for a place but I had a stiff interview there and they wanted very high 'A' level grades, so in the end I settled on Liverpool.) No one thought it strange to have someone like me around for, by a remarkable coincidence, there was a youngster named Mark Palios who was taking a degree in psychology at Manchester University on the books at the same time. He had to put up with all the taunts and jibes but survived well enough, playing for Tranmere from the 1973–74 season until his transfer to Crewe Alexandra in 1979–80. He went back to Prenton Park three years later and still successfully combines his professional football with a thriving business in Liverpool. Both Mark and I were in the squad which travelled north of the border for pre-season practice matches against a Motherwell side managed by Ian St John – East Fife and Kilmarnock. I was even given half a game against East Fife, causing no great stir as an ineffective striker.

Although I was very much an amateur I was treated as a first-year professional, playing for the reserves in the Northern Floodlit League mid-week and for the 'A' team on Saturday in the Lancashire League. I increased my tally to three games a week when my first term began at university as I played for my department team. I helped with the chores at Prenton Park but drew the line at cleaning the senior professionals' boots. Although it would have helped the club had I done so, the management respected my self-imposed demarcation line between the amateur and the apprentice professionals. I always cleaned my own boots at Tranmere and continued to do so until the last couple of years at Manchester United when laziness saw me join the ranks of the pampered professional.

I wasn't the only one to differentiate between amateurs and professionals. Trainer Johnny King taught me a salutary lesson during that pre-season training period when he stopped play because I was laughing at something that was happening off the pitch. He tore a strip off me, saying that while I might be an amateur the other guys were trying to earn livings to support their wives and kids and that it was not a laughing matter. I realised immediately that he was right and I was wrong and that lesson stayed with me for the rest of my professional career. That was still a while coming but I became aware, in the meantime, that those professionals in the first team at Tranmere were not very far ahead of me. I was no Incredible Hulk, but I had somehow managed to sprout seven or eight inches in my last year or so at school. I was no longer the smallest kid in the class but it still took me a while to realise and appreciate the fact that I could now shoulder other players off the ball.

I wasn't working terribly hard in my first year at university and had no problems in fitting in my lectures and studies with my football and training at Tranmere Rovers. I still found time to go and see Liverpool at Anfield and even to watch my brother Kevin play for a fibre glass company called Fazaplaz in the Liverpool Business Houses League. They even persuaded me to play once or twice. I will never forget the day the man who ran the team asked me to check the medical kit before a game. It was a huge wooden affair with a big red cross painted on it but when I opened it all that was inside was a sponge. It looked professional, which was all that mattered.

I eventually made my début for the Tranmere first team in the semi-final of the Liverpool senior cup against, of all teams, my own favourites Liverpool. It was not even their reserves though I do remember that Jimmy Case played against us at Prenton Park and around 500 people turned up for the morning kick-off to see us reach the final with a 3–2 win. I didn't do too badly for an 18-year-old playing his first game, in fact a damned sight better than I did against Everton in the final, and I then found myself in the senior squad.

It was an eye opener even though I was only there as thirteenth man. To say I was raw would be an understatement and not even life at university had been much help as I discovered on the way back from one of those early games at Hereford. Johnny King asked me what I wanted to eat on the return journey so that the order could be telephoned ahead. I hadn't a clue what style of food they ate but I overheard a couple of the team asking for steaks and I did the same. 'What kind of steak do you prefer,' asked the trainer King, 'and how do you like it cooked?' I hadn't got a clue what he was talking about. My diet in those days mainly consisted of egg and chips and though my Mum had cooked me steaks in the past, no one had told me what sort they were and I just ate them as they came. It wasn't until that day in Hereford that I learned there were different cuts of steak such as sirloin, rump and fillet. Thankfully Johnny King kept quiet about that particular gap in my education and I was spared the inevitable ribbing I would otherwise have received from the players.

Despite the social gaffes it was a good way to start off 1974 and I made my League début against Aldershot in a Sunday game at Prenton Park wearing the number seven shirt. The team that day comprised: Johnson, Mattias; Flood; Veitch; Yeats; Seasman; Coppell; Stevenson; Moore; Young; Tynan; and Sub. Palios. It should have been memorable but it wasn't. I can't even remember the score other than that we lost. Aldershot, however, were to figure strongly in my future for it was against them the next season that I scored my first League goal and Tranmere were scheduled to play against them the day I first played for Manchester United 75 hours after signing. However, to have considered such a turn of events then would have been nothing short of ludicrous for while I continued with my first-year studies I made just six first-team appearances in that season.

The important thing was that I was learning about the game. I was fortunate to have some seasoned professionals around me and a manager in Ron Yeats who had been schooled in the best of habits at Anfield. Although we were a small club with few resources and precious little money, big Ron Yeats insisted that everything should be done properly and I would not be exaggerating if I suggested that I owed a great deal of the successes that were to follow to him. He was intent on giving youth an opportunity and under another manager I may have never been given my chance in what was a struggling team and when I was, I had people like Willie Stevenson, another Liverpool favourite, on hand to offer practical advice.

Ron Yeats tried to run Tranmere like a miniature Liverpool. It was very professional, the training was based on the type he had experienced at Anfield and when we went away we stayed at the best hotels and ate the best meals. The difference lay in the quality and ability of the players around him. The whole club was organised around 17 or 18 players. I was probably given more publicity than I should have been in my first season as, suddenly, it became fashionable around Merseyside for footballers to be well-educated, supposedly in contrast to the usual trend, with Brian Hall and Steve Heighway at Liverpool and Mark Palios and me at Tranmere. It led to any number of interviews with journalists who were eager to discover how I trained away from the club and this earned me the not unpleasant reputation of being the new 'Kevin Keegan'.

I could hardly tell them that my favourite form of training was to kick a ball against a wall just as I had done when I was a kid and, instead, I told them that I had worked out my own routine from two coaching manuals I had at home, Alan Wade's *Preliminary Coaching Badge Manual* and Tommy Docherty's *Teach Yourself Soccer*. That sounded much more impressive as did my 45 minutes of yoga each day to get rid of that muzzy feeling from studying all day.

Any university student would tell you that most of the work is done in a mad panic just before the examinations, not only in the first year but all the way through the course. I suppose I could have balanced out my work better but it suited me that way. Three terms of ten weeks each leaves an awful lot of spare time and a lot of the lads took part-time jobs to help supplement their grants. Football was not only a good distraction but also provided an extra few pounds to make student life that little bit easier. Had I not been involved with Tranmere I would have probably fulfilled a desire to work as a Butlin's Red Coat. I did, in fact, eventually get to work for the holiday company after I was forced to retire, coaching football at four camps in the space of five days which cured me of that private ambition for life!

With my comparative wealth and extra height I also had a little more confidence concerning the fairer sex. Not that I went mad making up for lost days as so much of my time was spent concentrating on my studies and football, not to mention the odd night out with the lads, but I did meet a pretty girl, a year younger than me, named Jane Humpreys who is now, I'm pleased to say, my wife.

I was becoming more certain of myself and after another pre-season jaunt to Scotland and a successful League Cup result I was more than a little peeved at being left out of the opening League game against Bournemouth. We lost and, ironically I had my first taste of professional gamesmanship at Selhurst Park. It was August and a scorching hot day and even so the heaters were on all day in our dressing room. But all that concerned me was to keep my place.

Although Tranmere were struggling I was quite happy with the way things were going for me in midfield and so was our manager Ron Yeats who told the local paper: 'You can play him anywhere. We know he's an upfield player but he is so strong we play him in midfield. He will finish up as an attacking player because he has got what a lot of full-backs – and any defender – hate, and that's speed and control. He has got a big heart as well. His finishing could be better but he reads play well and he can go past people with the ball. When he's here full-time it's great. When he goes back to university he loses a wee bit of fitness.' Ron Yeats' assessment of my game was very perceptive, but he was wrong about my fitness because I played such a lot of games and ran a great deal when I was on my own.

I felt I was making good progress and the highlight of my time at Tranmere came when we were drawn against First Division West Ham in the League Cup. We drew 0–0 and were unlucky not to sneak a surprise win. As we came off the pitch Graham Paddon came over, put his arm around me and said: 'Keep playing like that and someone will pick you up.' It gave me a great boost and I have felt a bond with Graham ever since.

We were quickly brought back to earth in the replay. I almost missed it when, a few days before we were due at Upton Park, I went into a tackle with Brian Horton at Port Vale and came out the worst with a badly cut instep. I only passed a fitness test at the last moment and rather wish I hadn't for we were hammered 6–0. To make matters worse I caught an early train back north to take my driving test and, needless to say, I failed. It served me right. I thought I had been clever in electing to take my test in Birkenhead rather than in the more familiar surroundings of Liverpool because there was a much shorter waiting list. I was driving my Dad's big Ford Consul and when I tried to reverse I finished with the car sideways on in the middle of the road. I didn't need the examiner to tell me that I had failed.

These, fortunately, were only minor hiccups and I was not only always in the side but I also managed to become the leading goalscorer. The only problem was that all was not going well for the team in general. Even our poor position in Division Three turned to my benefit because it gave me the opportunity to work with the manager I admired above all others – the legendary Bill Shankly.

He had relinquished the reins at Anfield and responded to the cry for help from one of his old stalwarts, Ron Yeats, to try and help us out of our predicament. What a thrill it was when the great man turned up at training one day, and just his being there helped. 'Shanks' possessed great presence and charisma and this was well illustrated when he travelled with us to an away game at Gillingham. This was always a difficult game and was made harder by the fact that we had not won an away game all season.

When we arrived at Gillingham station there was no coach waiting for us and we had to make the short journey to Priestfield Stadium on foot. It could reasonably be expected that one of the world's most respected managers would take a cab but not a bit of it. There he was striding out with the lads, filling us with confidence the way no one else could. The magic worked, I scored and we won.

When I think back that trip could have been a total disaster, for had we lost we would have been further demoralised on the return journey when we arrived back at British Rail to discover that the restaurant car we had booked had not been provided. There was not even a buffet for a sausage roll or a sandwich, much less a bottle of lager with which to celebrate. We accepted it but not Shanks. He went absolutely beserk, pinning the hapless guard in a corner where he proceeded to give him a piece of his mind. 'These lads,' he growled in that memorable Scots accent, 'have just played their hearts out, given blood for their club and you cannot even come up with a good excuse. You and British Rail are a disgrace to mankind.' It carried on in that vein until Shankly left the man a quivering wreck and then, as a parting shot, he turned back and sneered: 'You deserve to be shot . . . with heavy bullets.' It didn't get us even a bag of crisps but it certainly made us all feel a lot better with a glimpse into the great man that we had only read about before.

He was especially kind to me and, apart from comparing me with Kevin Keegan, he told the papers: 'He is quick, has good movement, and a lot of courage. He can play on the right side, in the middle, or with a roving commission. Given the right kind of club he has all it takes to become a very good player, a real proposition. He is a great player in the making – like Kevin in so many ways. If I was still at Liverpool, he'd be in my team.'

I was immensely proud to be spoken of like that. It also meant that other clubs were sitting up and taking notice and, for the first time, I was really beginning to think I could make a living from football. My thoughts were reinforced by newspaper speculation and by Ron Yeats telling me that Liverpool, Everton or some other club were in the stand watching me. As a result it started to take me 10 or 15 minutes to settle into the game and at the most important stage of my career I began to produce my worst football. Fortunately it did not put everyone off. When the chance came it was completely out of the blue, so much so that, at first, I thought the whole thing was a send-up. I was at home studying when the telephone rang and it was Tranmere's General Manager Dave Russell to tell me of Manchester United's interest. I had never spoken to Dave on the phone and I suspected that it was one of the club comedians, such as Tommy Young, taking the micky after all the newspaper talk.

The rest of the team had already departed for Aldershot for five days' training at the army camp in preparation for their Third Division relegation battle when Dave Russell told me to report to Prenton Park on Tuesday lunchtime to meet Tommy 'the Doc' Docherty, the larger-than-life manager of top of the Second Division Manchester United. At that time I was on a part-time wage of £10 a week but when I arrived at the ground Dave Russell pulled me to one side to tell me that they had told the 'Doc' that I was earning treble that figure.

Naturally I had thought of little else other than playing for United since that first telephone call and I had already made up my mind that I was going to sign for Manchester United if offered a contract and, if necessary, give up my university course to do so. The Doc quickly made it clear that there were no doubts on his part and when he asked me how much I was earning, I told him £30, and he promptly replied that if I would sign a two-year contract he would double it. It was only later that I realised that this had been done for effect and had I said that I was earning £50 a week Doc would have still offered to double it.

The Manchester United manager told me that my contract would be ready and waiting for me to sign at Old Trafford next day and that I was to go home and think it over. As if I needed to! My mind was made up and the only difficulty was that I hadn't a clue whereabouts Old Trafford was in Manchester and, now that I had passed my test, I didn't fancy trying to find my way there in my Austin 1100. Happily Dave Russell gave me a lift to the ground where I told Tommy Docherty that I was ready to sign and that I was prepared to give up my studies. He wouldn't hear of it, insisting that I should carry on and get my degree but to train with United.

The business was completed by midday and the Doc looked at his watch and casually remarked that as he was thinking of making me substitute against Cardiff that Saturday it might be an idea if I joined the scheduled practice match that afternoon. I hastily told him that I wasn't ready, that I hadn't slept and that I hadn't got my boots with me but he brushed all excuses aside and within hours of signing I was playing for United reserves against the first team.

God knows what my new team-mates must have thought of this player from the depths of the Third Division because I didn't get a kick for the full match. It was nothing to do with playing for the reserves because there were plenty of good players like Tommy Baldwin and Ron Davies playing alongside me; it was just that I never got involved. I could have been crucified but no one said a word and coach Paddy Crerand told the waiting newspaper men how well I had done.

A new future had opened up in front of me overnight, though I felt a twinge of regret at leaving little Tranmere at such a crucial time and, indeed, they were relegated at the end of that season and Ron Yeats was sacked when it became obvious that they would be. The big man deserved more than that after working with such limited resources but it is a risk every manager takes when he accepts the job. I was sold because the gates had dipped below 3000 at Prenton Park and Tranmere needed the cash to pay their bills. It was decided that United would pay £40,000 down and a further £20,000 after I had made 20 first team appearances for them. The story went round that United settled the difference after only four games but I fancy that this was a bit of propaganda for the benefit of the media.

Dave Russell revealed in the *Liverpool Daily Post* that United had been trying to sign me for some time, stepping up their bid after Tranmere's three defeats in four matches. He told the paper: 'It is a wonderful chance for him. Who wouldn't want to join United? It's something that is inevitable with a club like us. It keeps us going. We have got to keep doing it. We have not sold a player for three years and gates have been getting steadily worse. How else can we pay the bills? It is simple logic. In any case, we have not been winning with Coppell in the side.'

It was an eye opener to read what was said about me, particularly the story of how I had been 'discovered' by Tranmere scout Eddie

Edwards. He claimed he had first found me playing on a park pitch at Aintree, adding: 'Although he was small I was impressed by his ability. You are always on the look-out for players who have a certain edge to their game. You don't find many of them but Steve impressed me because he made up for his lack of height by his great tenacity. He showed he was a terrier for hard work and was dangerous coming forward from midfield.

'I watched him in several other park games to check his progress, but he never knew I was there, who I was or what I was doing. This is part and parcel of scouting . . . you keep yourself to yourself and your cards close to your chest. Even now I doubt that Steve knows how Tranmere came to sign him. Eventually I recommended him to Tranmere manager Ron Yeats and after the club had been impressed with him in a trial he signed amateur forms and was only 16 when he made his first team debut in a pre-season friendly against East Fife.' Apart from the fact that I was 18 and not 16 when I first played for Tranmere the comments were extremely illuminating and Eddie was right, I didn't know how I had been selected until he spoke to the newspapers.

It seemed that the only person not totally delighted by my move from Tranmere to Manchester United was the Third Division club's chairman Bill Bothwell who complained: 'We sold him for less than we thought he was worth. But it is the need that makes the market.' All the same it almost doubled the club's earlier record when they had sold goalkeeper Jimmy Cumbes to West Bromwich Albion for £35,000 in 1969. However, the spiralling transfer market was soon to wipe my name from the Tranmere record books as Ronnie Moore went to Cardiff city for £120,000 in February, 1979.

It was almost as if all this was happening to someone else as I read about myself in newspapers other than the *Birkenhead News* and the *Liverpool Echo* with photographers even waiting outside the local cinema to take pictures of my girlfriend Jane and me going in to watch *Earthquake*. Before I knew it I was pulling on a red number 12 shirt and warming up with United in front of a packed Old Trafford. I could hardly believe it as I sat on the substitutes' bench with Tommy Docherty watching *my* team playing Cardiff City.

6

Magnificent Manchester United

I am not sure whether Manchester United were ready for my somewhat rapid and largely unexpected début – certainly I was not the best prepared footballer to pull on one of those famous red shirts. The programme for that game on 1 March, 1975, against Cardiff City, which went on sale to the 43,601 who filled Old Trafford, showed the team as: Stepney; Forsyth; Houston; Greenhoff; James; Buchan (captain); Morgan; McIlroy; Pearson; Macari; Daly and substitute Kopel. However, the oversight did not lessen the thrill, far from it for Frank Kopel had played for United a few years previously and because of the similarity in our names I had often identified myself with him.

In any case, who was I to complain. I was in a total daze and even now the events of that day are still hazy, though I remember getting lost on my way to the ground and having to stop in Eccles and ask for directions before I arrived late for the pre-match meal at the Lancashire County Cricket Ground. Worse still was the fact that I did not have a pair of boots to play in! That, however, was not entirely my fault. We didn't have a lot of kit at Tranmere and my boots were gone, with the rest of the team's equipment, to Aldershot. Fortunately Stuart 'Pancho' Pearson took the same size and he lent me an old pair of his.

I cannot remember much else of what happened in the dressing room before the game, nor even the kick-about in front of the heaving mass of bodies they call the Stretford End but what will stay with me for the rest of my life was running onto the pitch for the first appearance. The score was 0–0 with half an hour to go and after one United victory in the last seven games only, the crowd were getting a little restless. I was warming up when we won a corner and was told to go on. I could vaguely hear a section of the crowd booing the decision to bring off one of their favourites, Willie Morgan, but all that concerned me was the fact that I was going to play. It was one of those moments when your stomach is in your mouth and you feel so elated that could jump the stand. I experienced that sort of emotion only twice again in my career and that was on my England début and in my first FA Cup Final. It is very easy to become addicted to the thrill of competition.

The occasion could, of course, have gone flat but, incredibly, it did not. It was the sort of début which would have been tossed aside as too unlikely by writers for kids' comics. As I ran towards the penalty area the corner was taken and before I had even reached it, Stewart Houston had scored. Better was to follow for, with my first touch, I crossed for Pancho Pearson to add the second. My next touch was a total mis-kick in the penalty area but such was my luck that it ran straight to Lou Macari who put us four up, Sammy McIlroy having scored the third in between. We came off 4–0 winners to the rapturous applause of the United faithful.

I shook hands with my Dad in one of those moments cherished by a father and son, and went into the dressing room on cloud nine. The down-to-earth Martin Buchan brought me abruptly back to reality when, in all innocence, I asked him if I could borrow his shampoo. He muttered something under his breath and turned away, leaving me surprised to say the least. Alex Stepney overheard and quietly explained that I had picked the wrong person. Martin's shampoo was private property!

I stayed in the side and my luck held out as United completed their season in the Second Division with an unbeaten run which clinched the Championship and ensured that they would be back where they belonged – in the First Division. I soon discovered that I had not suddenly acquired supernatural powers. My next game was in the local derby with Bolton Wanderers at Burnden Park and though we won it with a goal from Pancho Pearson, I not only missed an absolute sitter but also picked up my first caution as a professional footballer. It may not sound a particularly serious offence but I held two rather unusual ambitions: the first was to appear as an amateur in the Football League and the second was to go through my career without being booked.

The latter aim stemmed from my days of watching Liverpool full-back Chris Lawler, a man who had not an ounce of malice in his body. He went for years without being booked, only to suffer a sudden inexplicable spate of them. I wanted to go one better but, in the derby against Bolton, I was told by Tommy Docherty to line up our defensive wall whenever there was a free kick near our penalty area. I was doing this when I vaguely heard the referee tell us to get back ten yards but when I turned around Peter Willis was taking out his book and I was cautioned for ungentlemanly conduct and two penalty points were marked against my name by the Football Association. I often thought about this when Peter became Chairman of the Referees' Association at the same time that I was asked to become Chairman of the Professional Footballers' Association.

The Bolton match was one of four occasions on which I was cautioned – and I disagreed not only with that one but also with two of the others. I was extremely annoyed when Kevin McNally took my name for time wasting when United were playing at Everton. It was bad enough that it was only the first half and we were leading 2–0 at the time but the referee knew me well from the days when he had trained with the Tranmere team. He told me afterwards that if I appealed against it I would get off but I didn't bother. The other time I felt I was mistakenly booked was at West Bromwich Albion and I maintain to this day that I was fouled and as I pitched forward I grabbed the ball in my hands.

It is, however, swings and roundabouts for I should have been sent off at Brighton in the 1982–83 season. To make matters worse the television cameras were there to witness me completely lose my temper. We were fighting hard to stay in the First Division title race at the time and had slipped a goal behind against the run of play. We bombarded Brighton but simply could not get that vital breakthrough. As the minutes slipped by Brighton, and striker Peter Ward in particular, wasted as much time as they could with Ward keeping the ball near the corner flag and winning three successive throw-ins. I had had enough. I kicked him as hard and as high in the air as I could and as the referee ran towards me I held up my hands and admitted that I had lost my temper. The official reached in his pocket for his book and as he took his pencil out from the top of his sock he told me: 'That was a sending-off offence – but as it is you I will let you off with a booking.'

Despite my booking and my glaring miss at Bolton, matters went exceptionally well for me in that first season at United. Although I was training only once a week with the rest of the team because of my continuing studies, I fitted in quite well and played to a reasonable standard in those last ten games. I was inspired by the good players around me and they helped me improve. I have noticed over the years that this can also work the other way with seemingly good players dropping down a division and struggling. I suppose the art of management is really sensing which players will be able to develop and raise their standards and recognising which ones are already playing to or beyond their capabilities because of those around them.

The season was also made easy by the fact that every game was a celebration as United headed back to Division One. The crowds were sensational with: 56,202 turning up at Old Trafford for the 1–1 draw with Norwich City; 46,802 for the 2–1 victory over York; 56,618 for the 3–2 win over Oldham Athletic; 52,971 to see Lou Macari's goal beat Fulham; and, finally, in the last match of the season against Blackpool, 58,769. All this time I was dying to get my name on the scoresheet and wondering just what it would feel like. I eventually managed to scramble one against Oldham and the match was a bit special. Another ambition achieved.

United was, in every sense, a very happy club and, at the same time, very down to earth. Although I was rarely at the ground there was no antagonism shown towards me, not even from the man I replaced, Willie Morgan. The newspapers made a song and dance about it at the time and Willie had a lot of friends among the supporters who felt he had been unfairly treated, especially as he had played in all 32 League games up to my arrival. Certainly some friendly rivalry existed between us and it was not until later, after he had first left the club, that we found we were ill at ease in each other's company but I was not aware of any undercurrents in my first season. And now the problem has been completely erased by time.

My particular friends in the 1975–76 season were Brian Greenhoff and Sammy McIlroy, probably because all three of us used the reserve team dressing room before training until we were promoted to the first-team dressing room the following season. The same tradition still applies and it is not a bad thing that you have to earn a place in one of football's most famous dressing rooms.

It was during these first few weeks that I began to suffer a little stomach trouble. Our regular physiotherapist, Laurie Brown, was away having a back operation and Jack Crompton had taken over his duties. During the Easter break from University I was at the club all the time and keen to soak up the atmosphere. I took the opportunity to ask Jack if he had anything for an upset tummy. He examined me, prodding around to discover the tender spots and, within an hour, I was in hospital being attended to by the eminent consultant, Sidney Rose, a Manchester City director. He confirmed that I had a grumbling appendix and decided to keep me in overnight, after which he announced that he would take it out the day after the season finished,

I couldn't help reflecting how different all this was from Tranmere where we had a physiotherapist who worked part-time for the club, coming into Prenton Park for half an hour during his lunch break. It seemed to me that these top players at United were wrapped in cotton wool. Not that there was anything especially professional about the team or set-up at that time. Trainer Tommy Cavanagh used to go on about our lack of sophistication and that was certainly the case with me. My tactics were the same whoever I played against in those early days – knock it past him and run. I needed only half a chance to cross the ball and I would smash it into the middle. If anyone had tried to tell me about being the third man in a running triangle I wouldn't have had a clue what he was talking about. Our manager Tommy Docherty totally backed my early style of play. We were encouraged to go forward and go for goal, there was never negative thought and no one told you off if you made a mistake. We simply went out in every game convinced that we were better than the opposition and that we could always score more goals than them.

United were a smashing side starting from the back with our goalkeeper Alex Stepney. When I first arrived at the club I considered him to be a potential weakness. I quickly discovered that he was very special and that his anticipation was better than any other goalkeeper's I have played with or against. Our skipper Martin Buchan as an absolute thoroughbred and in that first year and the next two seasons in Division One, I doubt whether there was a better central defender in the country. Sometimes he was a difficult character to fathom and his dry sense of humour often left you wondering whether he was serious or just having a quiet laugh. Buchan was the same with everyone, even the Press. There was one memorable day when he came out of the dressing room after a game to be asked by a journalist if he could have a quick word. 'Aye,' he responded without breaking stride, 'Velocity.'

Buchan was a very private person and few knew of the tremendous work he did for charity. He would always be pushing over a pile of pennies for the blind or visiting sick children in hospital and a day never passed when he didn't bring in an autograph book and say to one of us: 'Sign this for a little blind boy, you're his favourite player.' Despite his reluctance to lend me his shampoo, I will probably keep in touch with Martin Buchan for the rest of my life.

In that season in the Second Division and the next two in the First Division, Martin was probably one of the most talented central defenders in European football. I was also a fan of Sammy McIlroy, who was dramatically underestimated, while Lou Macari and Gerry Daly were the engine room around which the team revolved. Lou was quite a practical joker. He was always up to some mischief or other and you would never know what was going to happen next with him. Fortunately I did not suffer nearly as badly as our other winger Gordon Hill, who was to join us the following season, for Lou would have him visiting local radio stations for fake interviews and even have him giving them over the telephone – to Lou, of course.

The character swept right through the team. Stewart Houston was a great athlete and club man, while Alex Forsyth was of great entertainment value with his huge clearances upfield and his admonishment to us forwards to 'get on the end of that'. Up front Stuart Pearson was lethal and, like Sammy, not fully appreciated by those who watched him. They would forget the massive part he would play in the build-up, as well as the goals he scored (18 of them that season). He had a perfect physique for football and was not afraid to go in where it hurt. He took a tremendous number of knocks and eventually the accumulation of those blows forced him to quit. I hope those who thought he was a shirker swallowed their words when he had to stop playing, because he was a winner.

It all kept bubbling along. There were few team talks and the training was often limited to lively games of five-a-side in which goalkeeper Stepney was the goalscoring star and the captain's first choice when teams were selected. As for strategy our only speciality was to come rushing out of defence to ensnare opposing forwards off-side but we scarcely needed to employ special tactics. A classic example was our final game of the 1975 season. It was against nearby Blackpool on 26

April, a beautiful summer-like day which saw nearly 59,000 people cram into Old Trafford and many more dangerously perched on the stand tops, including one rash United fanatic named Ashley Grimes who, of course, was later to play for the team he loved so much. Ashley and the other United supporters were rewarded by a runaway four-goal victory with Pancho scoring twice and Macari and Brian Greenhoff adding the others. As we trotted back to the half-way line after one of the goals, Blackpool left-winger Mick Walsh looked around at the jubilant masses on the terrace and turned to me and said 'It just wouldn't be right if we beat you today.' It was then that it struck me that instead of going into Division Four with poor old Tranmere I was going to Division One. What a difference a few days can make.

It was over and we were up, three points clear of second-placed Aston Villa and eight ahead of third-placed Norwich City. Some of the players were off to take part in international matches, the remainder were going on a celebratory, money-making world tour while I had a date with Sidney Rose to have my appendix removed in hospital and then exams at university. I took my books to hospital, swearing to myself that I would begin my revision just as soon as the Doc and Tommy Cav left for the tour with the rest of the team – I couldn't wait for them to go as my sides ached for hours afterwards from the jokes they cracked on their visit.

I scraped through my exams that year as, typically, I had left everything until the last moment. It was with great relief that I finished the last paper and with some trepidation I then faced the prospect of my first-ever flight on an aeroplane 48 hours later to join up with the rest of the Manchester United squad in Hong Kong. The result was that I finished up getting extremely drunk on one of the few occasions in my life.

My pal and I had a real skinful and, encouraged by the booze, we planned to go back to the girls' quarters at the university hall of residence, pretend we were liaison officers and see who we could chat up. Luckily for us we managed to get no further than the cemetery in Aigberth Road before the taxi driver threw us out of his cab. Worse was to follow for as we struggled to pull ourselves together a police car stopped and we were on the verge of being picked up for being drunk and disorderly. Wouldn't that have made a good story for the tabloid newspapers – United's university student thrown in jail on the eve of his first tour! Fortunately my mate was by then being violently sick and presumably the officers did not want to run the risk of his being ill in their car and so they told me to get him home – or else. Easier said than done and my solution was to push him over the church wall into the graveyard and follow him over. After collapsing on the other side, we both fell into a deep sleep and I woke up shivering – and alone. My mate was nowhere to be seen. I managed to get home where I tele-phoned him to see what had happened. Would you believe it, even in his appalling drunken state, he told me he had managed to chat up a young lady waiting for a taxi at a bus shelter.

I just had time to pack and get myself in shape to catch the connecting flight from Manchester's Ringway Airport to Heathrow. I was com-pletely overawed by the size of the airport as well as by the aeroplanes themselves. For someone who had never been out of the country, the thought of being away for three weeks was quite an adventure and I admit that my knuckles were white on every take-off throughout the flight. Sir Matt Busby was supposed to be aboard but, in my anxiety, I didn't have time to think about him or anyone else until we took off from Bombay when I summoned up my courage and asked the senior steward if United's former manager was on board. He assured me that he would have known if such a VIP had been aboard as he would have been given the red carpet treatment. I eventually found Sir Matt at the back of the aircraft, amid the hubbub of the travelling Indian families, leaning back and calmly smoking his pipe just as though he was filming one of those television advertisements for cigars.

We arrived in Hong Kong to walk straight into the middle of a row between the players and the manager. They had all been away for some while, especially those that had been on international duty, and they wanted to have their laundry cleaned by the hotel and at the club's expense. The Doc said that they must pay for it themselves. I couldn't understand why a club that had run so smoothly in those few weeks I had been with them should be fighting over such a minor problem. It was only four hours before kick-off when I arrived there and the Doc promptly asked me if I fancied playing. Keen as I was I had been in the air for almost 20 hours and, unused to the severe humidity, I felt like a limp rag and would have collapsed if I had played. I decided to wait until we reached Australia and I did not even have the energy to look around that big, bad, busy city.

The friction between the manager and the players increased when we reached Perth, Australia. The Doc was invited to take three players to compete in an important head-tennis competition. This was being widely promoted in Australia at the time; it was going to be the new in-sport and we were to help it take off. The manager asked Sammy McIlroy, Brian Greenhoff and me to take part for the sum of 150 Australian dollars each. When the other boys heard about the deal it was decided that all the money should go into the general pool, and though the fees were not much it would at least have paid the cleaning bills.

The three of us, considered to be the Doc's favourites, were used as pawns by the other players and Alex Stepney, Lou Macari and Martin Buchan were elected spokesmen for the rest of the squad. I wondered what the hell I had landed myself in and I had no hesitation in offering my cut to the pool. It was the one time that Doc and I did not see eye to eye. He must have thought that I had let him down and he turned on me, described me as a certain part of the female anatomy and said he would have me out of the club and down the road before my feet could touch the tarmac.

It was an uncomfortable and difficult moment for a new player. I telephoned home that night and told them, in all sincerity, that I wished that I had not come. I didn't expect it to be a holiday but, after the emotion of those final weeks of the season, I thought it would be a little more relaxed than it was turning out to be.

The sad thing about that trip for me was that I was far too näive to appreciate it or to take advantage of the opportunity to sightsee as we flitted from Hong Kong to Australia and New Zealand and then, as a special treat, one night in the Los Angeles downtown Hilton. The hotels and travel were like nothing I had experienced before, even the smells were different and I could smell Hong Kong on my clothes every time I opened my suitcase. I am ashamed to admit that I kept carefully to steaks and burgers and did not even try a Chinese meal. When we arrived in the States I decided to be brave. We had been told to use the exotic rooftop restaurant and order what we wanted. I steamed in and ordered 'Oyster Rockafellow' and some luxurious-sounding fish dish. I spat out the first oyster, that was a dozen of the expensive shellfish down the drain, and then discovered I did not like the main course either. I finished up back in my room ordering a sandwich and a glass of milk. Much of the rest of the time was spent sleeping off the jet-lag. Some international traveller!

The undercurrents of discontent on the tour, understandable when you have been living in each other's pockets for so long, was quickly forgotten when the 1976–77 season got under way. Whether it was that youthful lack of sophistication, tales of the unexpected or simply our ability, I do not know but we took that First Division by storm. I must confess that I was extremely apprehensive at the vast gulf between my limited experience and what awaited me in the First Division. I need not have bothered for, on a boiling hot day at Molineux, we beat a very ordinary Wolves with two goals from Lou Macari and then followed that by beating Birmingham City by the same score at St Andrews three days later with Sammy McIlroy doing the business with both goals.

I was not particularly outstanding at Wolves but helped save the critical situation against the Birmingham Blues when we lost goalkeeper Alex Stepney through injury. Brian Greenhoff went in goal and made a couple of fine saves and the whole team rose to the occasion. Everyone, however, was suspicious about our beginning, even when we followed our double-barrelled start by blasting five goals past Sheffield United in front of 56,000 fans in our first home game. It was said that we had played against average teams only, and that we would struggle when we met the best. Our detractors all had to change their tune when, after drawing at home with Coventry and beating Stoke away, we beat Spurs 3–2 at Old Trafford to stay top.

I was loving every moment. The full-backs didn't know me and didn't know what to expect. I even managed to score a couple of goals in one game against Arsenal and would have had my first hat-trick but for that remarkable goalkeeper Pat Jennings who made a terrific save over his right shoulder, tipping the ball round the post when I was already celebrating the goal. By early November I had scored four times and was beginning to fancy my chances, even after my room-mate Brian Greenhoff bet me I wouldn't get five, never mind the double figures I had in mind. Having achieved a boyhood ambition by scoring at the

Kop End against Liverpool (albeit when we were three goals down), I took him on. However, Brian was right – I didn't get another in the League and scored only one more in a League Cup tie against Brentford.

We did not quite maintain our early season momentum but we still did far better than our critics had predicted. They had forecast that we would get destroyed in the air at the back but, despite the lack of inches and teams throwing the ball into our box, Martin Buchan and Brian Greenhoff held rock steady and we never slipped out of the top five.

We eventually finished a good third behind the Champions Liverpool and Queen's Park Rangers, watched by more than any other club with over a million spectators, averaging 54,750 a week at our home games, while pulling in more people away from home than the other teams, including the Champions Liverpool. We were, by now, playing with two out and out wingers for manager Tommy Docherty had again looked in the lower divisions and had come up with the unpredictable Gordon Hill from Millwall. It wasn't only the fans who took notice of us for, in March 1977 both Gordon and I caught the attention of England manager Don Revie and we were picked to play for the Under 23s in the return leg of an UEFA Championship tie against Hungary. England had already lost the first leg 3–0 in Hungary but we almost pulled it back, losing 4–3 on aggregate. I felt very relaxed as my début was at Old Trafford where, once again, the fans responded magnificently with a record 33,410 turning up.

With egg-heads Brian Hall and Steve Heighway also doing well for Liverpool, I found myself in demand by the media. I was given a lot of television coverage and the BBC even arranged to come to Liverpool University to film me in my other role. The only problem was that there was a particularly attractive young lady by the name of Carolyn Hill in my seminar group and every time the cameraman scanned around the students he would zoom in on her and ignore me!

All I can say is that it would have ruined my image if the Press had got wind of my ignorance of the different cuts of steak or that I had been on the tour of Hong Kong, Australia, New Zealand and the States wearing blinkers, or that I had found the only straight massage parlour in Hong Kong! Of course there are some unintelligent footballers but there are also a good many bright ones – and not just those who have enjoyed higher education. Just because professional footballers, in the main, leave school at 15 does not mean that they cannot talk intelligently about politics, travel or current affairs. It is ridiculous to generalise about any group of people in the way footballers have been labelled. One of the reasons they have a bad name is because they do not outwardly appear to appreciate the chance of foreign travel professionals get with top clubs. You regularly read stories of how players look up from a game of cards on the coach to ask which country they are in now but European club or international football is all hit and run. You arrive in a city, go straight to your hotel, eat, sleep, train, play and go back home again. Sitting on a coach and sightseeing for hours is no preparation for a big game.

All our attention that first season, however, was concentrated on more domestic affairs and, apart from keeping pace with the challengers for the Championship, we also had the Cup competitions and what made the season really memorable for me was that we went all the way and reached Wembley to play in a Cup Final. My previous Cup success had been limited, to say the least, having helped Tranmere beat non-League Farsley Celtic at Leeds United's Elland Road ground. I scored in a 2–0 win.

There was little or no thought at the start of the season of how far we would go and even our initial victories over Third Division Oxford United (2–1 at Old Trafford) and Peterborough United (3–1 at Old Trafford) were not very memorable. A key factor was that we were now playing 4–2–4 formation, deploying two wingers in Gordon Hill and me. He had arrived in the middle of November and when the Doc signed him I felt that I was going to be axed from the side, particularly when Gordon sat in the stand at Maine Road to watch us lose by four goals to our local rivals Manchester City in the League Cup. It was my own inferiority complex rather than any newspaper speculation and I was worried simply because I was still very much a part-timer as I continued to combine my training with my university lectures and studies.

Gordon and I first played together against Aston Villa on a cold, wet November day in front of 51,682 fans who watched us win 2–0. That was to be our springboard to Wembley. By the time we played Leicester City in the fifth round at Filbert Street, Wembley had become a distinct possibility with little Lou Macari inspiring us to a 2–1 victory. He was at his peak that day, covering every inch of the ground. It is strange how little things stick in your mind and that day it was Lou's cry of 'Timpson's.' Intrigued, I asked him what it meant, not realising the connection with the famous chain of shoe shops. It meant 'Boot It' and it is an expression I picked up and have used ever since.

After that game snooker player and United fanatic Alex Higgins tried to get into the dressing rooms to offer his congratulations only to be stopped by the ever watchful Tommy Cavanagh. 'Who are you?' asked Cav suspiciously. 'I'm Hurricane Higgins,' said the Irishman. 'I couldn't care who you are, you're not coming in here,' said Cav slamming the door and he continued to do so to anyone who tried to gain entry in every round as we went on our way to Wembley. To his credit Alex took the hint and when we finally reached Wembley he sent each and every one of us a telegram with a little poem incorporating our names. It must have taken him ages to think them up and cost a fortune to send them but, even so, he never managed to get past Cav and into our dressing room.

However, we weren't too troubled by outside interference. Leicester were a good Cup side and by beating them we were suddenly given a chance. We looked as if we had blown it in the sixth round when Wolves, whom we had beaten so convincingly at the start of the season, held us to a 1–1 draw at Old Trafford and then went into a two-goal lead in the replay. It was funny how often during that season we would find ourselves a goal or two behind and yet ended up winners. I suppose it was because we always fancied we could score goals against any defence and this day was no exception. We came back to force extra time and when Sammy McIlroy scored the winner we behaved as excitedly as our supporters.

There we were, not only in the semi-finals but also chasing the League title. Instead of the critics asking when the bubble was going to burst, they now talked about us winning the 'Double'. The pressure had begun to mount and the Doc promptly called a meeting of the players to tell us not to become involved in any of the predictions and to keep a low profile. He told us that we would be subjected to enough pressure without mention of trophies. Tommy didn't follow his own advice for when we beat Wolves we already knew that we would have to face League Champions Derby County at Hillsborough while Second Division Southampton and Third Division Crystal Palace were contesting the other semi-final. Tommy was quoted as saying: 'This is the first time the FA Cup Final will have been played at Hillsborough – for what else can you call our semi-final against Derby? The other semi-final is a bit of a joke really.'

To prepare for the big semi-final we had booked into an hotel in Buxton before the game but when we arrived we saw how run down it was and the Doc immediately demanded to see his room first before the rest of us checked in. Sure enough the bed was not made up and the room was still dirty from its previous occupant. Doc was then shown another room which still had suitcases in it and he immediately ordered us back onto the coach and took us to Mottram Hall, the hotel we used before home games and where we knew we would be looked after. Mario, the head waiter at the old and charming Cheshire hotel, was keen on shooting, and the next day, Friday, the Doc decided he wanted to go with him and invited both Mario's regular shooting partner, Gordon Hill, and me to go along as his gun bearers. Tommy desperately wanted to use his gun and as soon as a couple of rabbits broke cover he was blasting away in all directions without getting near them. We traipsed over the countryside for hours trying to find our manager something to kill, finally giving up and heading back for our hotel where Tom, after a furtive glance around, let fly at the tame ducks on the ornamental pond. He even missed those.

It could have proved disastrous with a semi-final to play the next day for we had walked so far that Gordon and I were very stiff. I had an average game but fortunately for the Doc and Manchester United, Gordon proved to be the match winner with the two goals that saw us to Wembley while Southampton won a disappointing game against the Division Three giant killers from London, Crystal Palace.

Gordon was one of the best players I have ever seen as he was very intuitive and had a very handy knack for getting goals. He scored ten times in his first season – twice as many as the other Manchester United winger in half the games. He was certainly our trump card that day as we emerged from our role of underdogs to beat the reigning League Champions convincingly. The only time they gave us problems was when Francis Lee came on as substitute but we survived and were through to Wembley. It was hard to grasp that we were going to be part of a spectacle watched by millions around the world, a game that had had me glued to my television every May for ten or eleven years – whoever had been playing.

However, we had to put the Cup behind us as we continued our quest to add the League Championship to the Second Division title we had won 12 months earlier and it was not until 21 April, when we lost 2–0 to Stoke, that we conceded the race. It was hard for a young side to chase so much but as the fixture congestion grew so Doc loosened the reins and, between matches, we hardly trained – just played. The backlog caught up with us in the end. I injured my ankle in a 2–1 win over Everton and then had to sit and watch as we kept our hopes alive by beating Burnley two days later only to see them vanish against Stoke two days after that. Even then we had another game against Leicester making it four games in seven days. Some way to prepare for a Cup Final.

Increasingly nowadays, the six-week period between qualifications and the final is a perpetual chase for cash from whoever wants to be associated with the potential winners. There is always a big debate over the value of a players' Cup Final pool, especially now that the leading professionals earn such good money. In my opinion pools are a good thing if they are organised properly and they can, indeed, help build team spirit. We decided against employing an agent and decided to do the work ourselves and split everything equally. Rules had to be drawn up over the distribution of the television fees which is now automatic and also to make sure that other areas of the media did not try to bother us with silly photographs and other such distractions. Even so, some of the attention was an imposition but we were sensible about it, realising that it was, for most of us, the biggest day of our footballing lives. It didn't interfere too much with our football but it could have done if it had been handled badly.

As it was we did not make a lot of money. It was peanuts once you took into account the big tax bill we all received a year later. Players are reputed to make vast profits from the sale of their tickets but there was not a huge demand for a Manchester United against Southampton line-up. For me it was my first final with every chance that it could also be my last and I was determined that everyone that I wanted to go would be there, including a group of my university mates who hired a minibus for the trip south to London. That took my entire quota and a few more besides.

We were finally able to put pools, tickets and everything else behind us when we moved to our Cup Final headquarters at Sopwell House on the Wednesday evening. There was only us and even the Press were restricted to a single day's visit to conduct their interviews. For the remainder of the time we watched television, played Monopoly and were given lots of massage from the Celtic masseur Jimmy Steele who had been brought in specially by the Doc.

Our nerves began to jangle on the Friday, particularly when we watched the television preliminaries. I was worried because the media was placing so much emphasis on Manchester United's wingers and saying how important they were to the eventual outcome. However, I wasn't half as nervous as I thought I would be when the big day dawned. I have often read that players can remember little about a Cup Final because it all goes so quickly. I can appreciate what they mean for one minute we seemed to be leaving the hotel on our way to Wembley and the next it was all over. It was not a great game. Southampton full-back Rodrigues looked after Gordon Hill so well that the Doc substituted him for David McCreery in the second half while I was fairly well policed by David Peach. Sammy McIlroy headed against the bar and the Cup was eventually won near the end when Bobby Stokes ran into Jim McCalliog's pass to beat Alex Stepney. I thought at the time that the goal was offside and, having seen the replays on television, I still do.

For the record:

1 May 1976 Southampton 1 Manchester United 0
Southampton: Turner; Rodrigues; Peach; Holmes; Blyth; Steele; Gilchrist; Channon; Osgood; McCalliog; Stokes.
Manchester United: Stepney; Forsyth; Houston; Daly; Greenhoff; Buchan; Coppell; McIlroy; Pearson; Macari; Hill (McCreery).

The season which had promised so much just a few short weeks earlier had abruptly ended leaving us with nothing but, strangely, it did not feel too bad at first. At least I had a medal that said I had played at Wembley in a Cup Final, the most prestigious game of the season, my first in the senior division. It wasn't until some days later when the thought struck me that maybe I would never get the chance to play there again and that we had tossed away a marvellous opportunity against Second Division opponents. Others must have felt the same way for we had a good night at our banquet on the evening after the match. The Doc, making an effort to cheer everyone up, was in good voice, singing a sad Irish song about a soldier with Cav giving the encore.

Despite finishing the season empty handed it had nonetheless been amazing for me. There I was studying at university and playing for my department's team during the week, then playing in front of 50,000 people every Saturday. I even took my college books to our Wembley hotel as my finals were just a month after the Cup Final. The club were very considerate, with the Doc always encouraging me to keep up my studies and to pass my exams and none of the players objected to me missing the occasional training sessions they held. The Doc might not have been so pleased, however, had he known about my extra-curricular football at university. We even managed to reach the inter-departmental final where we lost 6–1. I played in goal and we had to keep it all very quiet with United going so well. It was a risky thing for me to do but the whole university would come to a halt every Wednesday for these games with everyone filing down to the pub afterwards. Thank goodness there were no photographers around when we played in that final or I might have found myself out of that rather more important final a few weeks later.

7

Under the Doc – Tommy Docherty

The media reckoned that there were half a million people waiting to welcome us back to Manchester the day after we had lost the Cup to the Saints. We travelled in an open-top bus and by the time we reached Albert Square the place was packed full with supporters hanging from every statue, and how they responded when Tommy Docherty promised them that next year we would be back and have the FA Cup with us. It was what they wanted to hear, typical Docherty bravado. They believed him because they wanted and needed to. After all wasn't this the man who had led their team back to the First Division and then to Wembley a year later. The players smiled, nodded in agreement and were happy that this pie-in-the-sky stuff was going down so well.

Who would have believed that it was a prediction that Old Moore himself would have been proud to foretell in his Almanac, but not even he would have possibly guessed what else would happen as Doc, in a matter of weeks of fulfilling his prophecy, was to be given a new contract – and then be sacked. Whoever said that football was a strange game must have had the Doc in mind. Tommy himself used to say that when one door opens, another smashes you in the face but on that May day in Manchester he honestly meant what he said and he was to repeat it so often throughout the next season that we eventually became convinced as well. Doc always maintained that if your name was written on the cup you would win it and he reinforced it by reminding us at regular intervals that you had to win only six matches to win the FA Cup.

The prophecies must have sounded a little hollow when we opened our account in the New Year, scraping past little Walsall and I personally had no thoughts of Wembley as I was taken off for playing so badly. Matters hadn't gone as well as they could have done for, after starting the season with great expectations, things had slipped. On 2 October we were top of the First Division when we lost the invaluable services of our outstanding skipper Martin Buchan. By the time he had returned to the side in December we had slumped to seventeenth place and we were still trying to pick up the pieces.

We could easily have gone quietly out of the competition in the fourth round when we met Queen's Park Rangers on a frozen Old Trafford pitch. We won by a single goal again, scored by Lou Macari, but it was one of those days when the home advantage is taken away by the underfoot conditions and it needs only luck to go against you and that is it. I suppose it was then that we began to feel maybe our name was written on the trophy after all.

By one of those great knock-out cup ironies we were given the opportunity to avenge our Cup Final defeat when, in the fifth round, the draw paired us with Southampton yet again, this time at the Dell instead of at Wembley. We drew the first game 2–2 to take them back to Old Trafford. It was a torrid match controversially refereed by Welshman Clive Thomas who helped us by sending off Jim Steele. For the first time in those two games I came face to face with Alan Ball and I immediately understood what his contemporaries meant when they talked of his commitment to the game. I was treated to one of those legendary fierce Alan Ball looks. His eyes were blazing and he seemed on the verge of exploding. You could sense his passion for the game.

However, fortunately, it takes all sorts to succeed at football, and in the replay it was a man who was the opposite of Ball in temperament and attitude, Manchester United striker Jimmy Greenhoff, who was to prove to be the match winner. One of the major changes to the team that season was when the Doc sold Gerry Daly to Derby County for £188,888 and spent £100,000 in bringing our defender Brian's elder brother from Stoke City. Jimmy was to take a little of the weight from Stuart Pearson's shoulders with Sammy McIlroy dropping back into the midfield spot vacated by Daly. Jimmy was a quiet fellow who got on with his job. In my opinion he was the best player I ever played with. There was no telepathy or anything like that, it was simply that whenever you needed him he was there. Unlike 'Bally' he was a quiet introvert and the fact that he never projected himself probably cost him international honours. It always amazed me that a player of his undoubted quality never won a cap. But on that day against

Southampton he scored both the goals that kept our interest alive.

All you can ask for when you reach the quarter-final stages of the FA Cup is that you are blessed with a home draw and, sure enough, Doc's predictions began to be realised as our name came out of the hat first against Aston Villa. In the match we were the best team, totally in control and deservedly won 2–1 at the first attempt and, in fact, there was not a single replay needed as we were joined in the semi-final draw by Liverpool, Leeds United and Everton. All we wanted then was to avoid Liverpool and even though we were the underdogs when we drew Leeds we were quite happy with the prospect of returning to Hillsborough. We had recovered our form in the League and another goal from Jimmy and one from me was enough to send us back to Wembley – just as Tommy Docherty had promised less than year before.

We were good value in that semi-final. Jimmy scored his goal from a Gordon Hill corner while I volleyed mine from the edge of the box as the ball bobbled invitingly. I did not see it go in but realised when I saw the crowd's reaction. They went wild and so did I. We had to withstand a lot of pressure in the second half to ensure another appearance at Wembley but we possessed the capacity to harass better sides out of their stride and Leeds were never to fulfil their potential. The main danger to us was their central defender Gordon McQueen, later to become a United player, and I remember standing in the hall-like area between the two dressing rooms before the game as he looked down on us from his great height and yelled that Leeds would crush the midgets.

Gordon plagued us from every dead-ball kick in that second half but Brian Greenhoff and Martin Buchan, as they had done so often that season, held firm and, though it became very frantic, we limited Leeds to a somewhat dodgy second-half penalty converted by Allan Clarke. We were jubilant as we returned to our dressing room and our day was almost complete when it looked as if Everton had beaten the all-conquering Liverpool side, only for referee Clive Thomas to disallow Bryan Hamilton's effort for handball. It meant a replay and, for the first time, I found myself at a Merseyside derby supporting Everton instead of Liverpool. We fancied ourselves against the Blues even though they had beaten us in the League Cup but we were not nearly so sure about beating a side which was sweeping all before them.

Liverpool won the game by three clear goals as they went in search of not only the League and Cup double but also the European Cup.

Neither the Doc, nor the team for that matter, were particularly cast down by the news. We were just delighted at getting a second chance so quickly and our manager said: 'This gives us an opportunity to put it right. I don't even mind if we lose as long as we do ourselves justice.' We had gathered momentum as the season progressed. After our initial slump due to the absence of Martin Buchan, we had recovered steadily and were able to challenge for a place in Europe. The arrival of Jimmy Greenhoff had given us balance while his brother Brian together with Martin ensured that we did not give many goals away. Following the passion of our first season back in the top division we were now working hard to improve our performance. The other teams had become used to our style of that first, joyous season and it was a question of us developing and consolidating our play.

Tommy Docherty was always convinced that we would win something and with time running out in the League – where we finally finished sixth – and a disappointing failure in the League Cup and the UEFA Cup, only the FA Cup remained. We had not had much luck with the draw in Europe for, having put out former European Champions Ajax of Holland in the first round, we then lost to Juventus in Italy. The League Cup was even worse because a lot of the top teams were put out early on and we really fancied our chances when we knocked in an incredible 17 goals in the first three rounds.

We began by beating my old club Tranmere 5–0 at Old Trafford. They certainly made it tough for us in the first half and I hardly had a kick as my old team-mate and fellow graduate Mark Palios followed me around the pitch like a shadow. We won easily enough in the end but needed three games before overcoming Sunderland in the next round. That, we thought, was the one that was sent to try us and we celebrated by crushing Newcastle United 7–2 at Trafford in the fourth round. Perhaps we became a little too cocky when we drew Everton at home but they brought us tumbling down-to-earth with a three goal beating.

Certainly we were not going to underestimate the other Merseyside team in the Final but because they were the favourites and going so well it took the pressure right off us. The fact that we had been to Wembley

Above The Liverpool Schoolboys Team 1965-66 which produced five professional footballers: *back row* Joe Gallagher (extreme right) and John Higham (third from the left); *seated* Peter Houghton (second from the left) and Billy Rodaway (fourth from the left) who is sitting next to the smallest member of the team, Steve Coppell

Below Tommy Docherty and I posing for the photographers at my graduation ceremony

Above Ron Atkinson has the ideal image
to lead a club of the stature of
Manchester United

Right Dave Sexton had the difficult job
of following Tommy Docherty only to
be let down by the players and harshly
criticised by the media. He is someone,
however, whom I will always respect

Below Tommy Docherty shows his
extrovert character as he leads the Cup
Final celebrations ably supported by Sir
Matt Busby *(right)* and Tommy
Cavanagh *(left)*

Above Left Bobby Robson took a while to make the transition from club to country and wanted to fill every minute he had with the players

Above Right Don Revie seemed to transmit his nerves to the players and even when he knew he was leaving for the United Arab Emirates everything still had to be right

Below Ron Greenwood was undoubtedly the most relaxed manager I played under and here, Terry McDermott, Phil Neal and Kevin Keegan all find something to smile about

Above Maybe not the tallest trio in the world but all played a big part in the development of the England team *(l-r):* Kevin Keegan, Ray Wilkins and I in Austria, 1979

Below Right Hotshot wingers Steve Coppell and Gordon Hill in Cheshire
Below Left Ron Greenwood was instrumental in bringing back wingers to the England team. Peter Barnes is on the left

Above My wife Jane and my mother Ena, the women in my life, don't know whether to support me or the FA Cup!

Below Making a hit record — one of three while I was at Old Trafford

Above I'd rather play with him than against him. The fearsome sight of former Leeds and England star, Trevor Cherry, now successful manager of Bradford City

Below The beginning of the end. England physiotherapist, Fred Street, has his first look at the injured knee which was eventually to put me out of the game

Above Dave Watson and I would often go and watch Status Quo in concert. This time Rick Parfitt gets his own back

Below I always took great delight in scoring against the Scots and was especially pleased with this one at Hampden Park in 1978 when Ally MacLeod described me as the worst player on the pitch

Above Left Martin Buchan, a thoroughbred footballer. *Above Right* One of my boyhood heroes at Liverpool and my first manager at Tranmere, Ron Yeats

Below Left Gordon Taylor, now Secretary of the Professional Footballers' Association. *Below Right* The Greenhoff brothers Brian *(left)* and Jimmy *(right)*, this time on opposite sides of the game between Leeds United and Manchester United

the year before also smoothed our path. The previous year we had been committed to doing too many things we did not enjoy and which weren't financially rewarding either. Spending the whole day at a shoe factory or a full afternoon having suits fitted was not on the agenda this time. We were relaxed, happy and in good spirits, and used an agent to ensure that we did not waste time with silly trying matters.

There were, of course, the usual scares leading up to the Final. We were all upset when poor Stewart Houston broke his leg at Bristol City just three weeks before the big game but we were fortunate in that we had a young Scot named Arthur Albiston who had played ten games or so. Then Martin Buchan was forced to miss some games and there was doubt as to whether he would be fit enough to play. He and goalkeeper Alex Stepney had taken some knocks and big Alex missed our last League game of the season at West Ham on the Monday before the final.

An example of just how relaxed we were in that week before the final was shown by the fact that the Doc took Gordon Hill and me to London the day before the West Ham game to do some advertising work with Gillette. He took us out to dinner that night at the Playboy Club where we enjoyed a bottle of champagne. It didn't seem to affect Gordon for he scored after just 25 seconds the next night though West Ham went on to win 4–2 and banish any lingering doubts of relegation.

We changed our Cup Final headquarters that year to the other side of London, staying at Selsdon Park in Croydon. It proved to be a good move for though we were further from Wembley it was far more secluded and we were not bothered by things like tickets. It was proving to be the most popular game of the season and a huge demand for tickets sent the price soaring on the black market. Every ticket I received had been requested well in advance for family and school-friends so, once again, the touts did not do at all well out of me. The only problem during the build-up was the doubt over Martin Buchan and, afterwards, our physiotherapist Laurie Brown admitted: 'I was particularly pleased to see him come through the game. On Wednesday he virtually had no chance of playing and it gave me great personal satisfaction to have got him fit in time.'

Liverpool had more on their minds for, having won the League title they were due to face the West German Champions, Borussia

Moenchengladbach, in the European Cup Final on the following Wednesday in Rome and because of their heavy commitments they were told that if the Cup Final was drawn on 21 May the replay would be on 27 June! The blunt-speaking Bob Paisley was quoted as replying: 'I am not an intelligent enough man to have the vocabulary to express myself at this stupidity.' But the team I had supported so devoutly as a kid were the undoubted favourites and such was their strength that Ian Callaghan was on the substitutes' bench.

Just as 12 months earlier, it was a very hot day and, recalling how dry my mouth had been on that previous occasion, I spent the morning drinking plenty of water. We left the hotel a good two hours before the kick-off and everyone was lively and feeling excited on the coach with reserves like Tommy Jackson and Paddy Roche helping it all along even though they were not playing themselves. We arrived to find we had been allocated the so-called lucky dressing rooms and we immediately set about convincing ourselves that this was the omen we needed.

Earlier that month Liverpool had beaten us at Old Trafford when Kevin Keegan had run wild. They honestly had seemed a much better side than us then – but it did not show at Wembley. Keegan, in particular, was kept in very close check by Martin Buchan, in fact I would go so far as to say he marked him out of the game. Buchan's feat can be put in perspective by Kevin's match-winning performance in Rome four days later when he took apart Berti Vogts, reputedly one of the world's best man-for-man markers, in a 3–1 victory.

A lot of critics blamed Ray Clemence for the first goal but, like him, I thought Pancho Pearson was going for the other corner and by the time he corrected, the pace of the ball at the near post was too much for him. It was, however, the goal the game needed and it sparked off a spell of three in five minutes. Liverpool hit straight back to score the equaliser and I felt I had let everyone down as Joey Jones dummied his way past me before crossing for Jimmy Case to beat Stepney. But, three minutes later, it didn't matter as we regained our lead with a goal that reinforced Doc's conviction that our name was written on that trophy.

Tommy Smith believed, and many agreed with him, that Jimmy Greenhoff had fouled him when winning possession. Jimmy's shot rebounded off a defender straight to Lou Macari whose instant reaction was to swing his left foot at it. It could have gone anywhere but it struck Jimmy Greenhoff on the chest and left poor Ray Clemence an unwitting spectator as it lazily curled into the opposite corner of the net. Liverpool sent on Callaghan for David Johnson, moving goalscorer Jimmy Case forward into an attacking position, but we responded by replacing Gordon Hill with an extra midfield player, Dave McCreery, and managed to hold on.

We had won and, having experienced the other result the season before, it needed no time to sink in. Everyone was very emotional with young Arthur Albiston, who had played so well, offering the injured Stewart Houston his medal. Stewart, typically, not only refused but described Arthur as the Man of the Match. However, for me that honour went to Martin Buchan, who had come so very close to not playing at all.

The banquet was at the Royal Lancaster but while Cav was Cav and loving every minute of it, the Doc was surprisingly quiet. At a time when you would have expected him to be triumphant and delighted with his renewed contract, signed on 1 May, he was quiet and restrained. He told the Press afterwards: 'I am still waiting for it all to sink in. I thought I would be doing handstands and cartwheels if we won, but in fact I feel absolutely drained of emotion at the moment. But I am delighted for all the players, particularly after the disappointment of last season.' Even his speech to us at the reception was low key and there were no songs or cabaret from him this time. The party was very nice but Doc's mood seemed to set the tone and, around midnight, Brian Greenhoff, Michael Docherty and I together with our wives and girlfriends slipped off to a Greek restaurant where we really let our hair down. When I say we had a smashing night I mean it quite literally for the house speciality was the quaint Greek custom of breaking plates. I was told later that because we broke so many, our bill should have come to more than £300, but because of winning the Cup we were excused.

United went on tour, Liverpool went on to win that European Cup and I set off on my first full England tour to South America. It was not until I returned that I discovered one of the reasons why Tommy Docherty had been so subdued at the banquet. By then the whole of football knew that he was having an affair with Mary Brown, wife of our physiotherapist Laurie.

I first heard the news on the car radio as I drove to my girlfriend Jane's house on my return from Gatwick Airport. I know there is a lot of heartbreak involved in a thing like this but my reaction at that moment was to burst out laughing. You see the players had known nothing of what had been going on and also Mary and Tom were complete opposites. I had met her only once or twice at social functions and my impression had been that she was a little reserved, maybe shy, and very well spoken, and in stark contrast to the ebullient Glaswegian who was always a bundle of fun and who was so wrapped up in football that he was quoted as saying: 'I talk a lot on any subject . . . which is always football.'

Laurie had once told us that Mary was more interested in horses than football and, to be honest, I thought at the time she was perhaps a little snobbish. To be frank my thoughts, as I continued the drive and digested the surprise news, were that Laurie would go and what a shame it was that it had happened. I did not think for a moment that it would be the manager who would be forced to leave but as the days went by it became more and more obvious that it was the Doc who would be on his way. That I did not find at all funny for if ever there was a man tailor-made to be manager of Manchester United it was Tommy Docherty. He was perfect for that club and it was as though all his earlier years of management in the game had been spent preparing for this one particular job.

When the Doc first arrived at Old Trafford he had said: 'No one will ever equal Sir Matt Busby's achievements and influence at Old Trafford, but I would like to go down as someone who did nearly as much . . . I'll be happy if at the end of the day people say, "well there could only be one Sir Matt . . . but Tommy Docherty came close to his standards and was the right man to follow on".' He was well on his way to acquiring such a reputation. He had been at the club for two and a half years and in that time Manchester United had gone from strength to strength: winning promotion to the First Division in the first season; finishing third in the League and reaching the Cup Final in his second; and winning the Cup in the third season. When I came back from South America I was convinced that we would be ready to take the First

Division title from Liverpool the following season. Although I had played so much football that season and then been on a long and tiring trip to Brazil, Argentina and Uruguay, I was itching to get started again, so confident was I of success. We had broken our duck in winning the Cup and the signs were promising.

Docherty loved the club and would have done anything for it. When he was finally dismissed all I could think was what a terrible waste. He was doing his job well and it wasn't even as if he had been neglecting his work for his affair; he even went to the Continent with the youth team for a tournament while speculation was growing. It was said that the Board sacked him because of pressure from the players' wives but that was rubbish. The running of Manchester United has nothing to do with the players' wives and they wouldn't have wanted to be involved anyway.

Tommy has taken a lot of criticism over the years for the things he has said and done but he accepted his dismissal with great dignity. Every newspaperman in the country was after his story and they besieged the house where he and Mary had set up home. The Doc told them: 'I have been punished for falling in love. What I have done has nothing at all to do with my track record as manager.' He could have earned a fortune selling his story to the Press, but he contented himself by adding, 'They sacked me as nicely as they could. It's one of the nicest sackings I have ever had.'

You speak as you find and so far as I was concerned Tommy Docherty and Tommy Cavanagh together were the biggest influence on my career as a professional footballer. I will always think of them as a pair, for they complemented each other so well. When the Doc was being fierce, Cav would soften the blow and when Cav went over the top, which he was prone to do, it would be the Doc who calmed things down. They were an impetuous couple but, on the whole, treated me fairly and helped develop my play and my career enormously.

As a Liverpool supporter when Tommy was the brash young manager of Chelsea, my impression of him was very different. They knocked my team out of the Cup and the Doc had had a great deal to say about it in the papers. What a big mouth, I thought, and that opinion grew and was emphasised with each of his ensuing jobs. As for United, being just 30 miles away from Merseyside, they were local rivals and I gained some perverse satisfaction when they were relegated. By the time I began playing professional football my opinion of him was beginning to change. He regularly appeared on a Granada television programme called *Kick Off* and watching him almost every week I formed an impression of a very tough, ambitious and down-to-earth man. I also had an inkling of a softer side from his laughing and joking on the programme. He was somewhat larger than life and when I was told by Tranmere that he wanted to talk to me I was both flattered and curious.

He was completely different from what I had expected. He was quiet and did not come across too strongly at all. If anything he was easy to get on with. He did not project himself but rather Manchester United, telling me that they belonged in the First Division and that I had a future with them – if I wanted it. There was no big sell and he took nothing for granted. I had told him that I was prepared to consider quitting my degree course if I went to Old Trafford full-time, but he would not hear of it.

During the first three months I spent at Old Trafford I rarely saw him. It was Cav who looked after the day-to-day running of the club and the training while Doc would now and then appear on the line to shout and bawl at us. He often used fairly basic language and he would also pick on individuals to criticise. But he was never predictable and when you expected a talking-to he would often be the opposite, sympathising and telling you to keep trying. That season, my first as a full-time professional, we won the Cup. With University over and done with, I was not playing as well as I had hoped. The Doc simply told me to get away for a few days to the Lake District which was a great tonic.

Doc's Gorbals tongue would often single someone out during a training session and be absolutely unmerciful, often for no apparent reason. I remember one day him picking on Dave McCreery and spending the whole morning criticising him. The next day Dave was expecting it to continue but it had all been forgotten and, in a way, the lad was motivated. It was possibly one of the ways he tried to encourage a player and I do not remember him holding a grudge nor having any particular favourites.

At times, however, he was inconsistent but, I suppose, this was linked to that element of surprise. He was never one to ponder a problem and would always make an immediate decision. He was impulsive both on and off the pitch and while an ordinary person would go into one of the instant tailors in Hong Kong to order a suit and a silk shirt to be made in a couple of hours, he would order four suits and a dozen shirts. It meant he could blow hot and cold and he was never too keen on being answered back. He demanded loyalty from his players and would take it as a personal affront if you disagreed with his ideas or policy. In return he was totally loyal to the then Chairman, the late Louis Edwards, of whom he thought the world.

He was also devoted to the United supporters. He once said that they could be a terrible embarrassment to the club and to him but that he would rather have them as an embarrassment than not at all. He would travel the world to meet and talk to branches of our supporters' clubs in places like Ireland and Malta, as well as throughout the United Kingdom. Just before I arrived at the club there had been bad trouble with the hooligan element of the fans and he responded by inviting them to the ground on Sunday mornings where he and the players would talk to them. It worked for you rarely hear of trouble of violence at Old Trafford any more.

I am certain he will spend the rest of his career searching in vain for another Manchester United. Ever since he was given the sack from Old Trafford he has been unable to find the same fulfilment. The club demands someone of a certain stature and he fitted the bill, and was able to pass on his enthusiasm to everyone at the club. That is why his time at United was like an unfinished symphony. It was not just my feeling that the club was on the verge of taking off when he left, a lot of us felt the same way and though nothing is certain in football, there would have been silverware to follow the FA Cup.

There were, of course, some grounds for his dismissal. Obviously the club thought long and hard about such an important decision and felt that they had certain standards to maintain. It was not just that he was having an affair but the fact that it was with the wife of one of the staff. However, managers are not made in heaven and, in the end, United were the biggest losers.

To describe a man like Tommy Docherty adequately is like trying to explain why you like a particular painting, different people see different qualities. I have, in the main, good memories of Docherty.

He flew back from a holiday in Malta especially to be at my graduation ceremony. He was marvellous, sitting at the back of the hall to watch the proceedings and then willingly posing for photographs with me afterwards. He was also one of the very first people to telephone when I had to quit the game and, within days, he was linking us together in management jobs. One in particular, at Stoke City, provoked particular interest with the Doc saying we were ready to take over together. It was the first I had heard about it. We had not even spoken! Had he asked me I would have given it serious consideration because I am sure I could have learned a great deal from the Doc and his unique style. So many of the things I say as a manager echo his words and phrases.

He was also a generous man. You would go to a function with him and suddenly champagne would be flowing. He gave his time freely and willingly to charity work, particularly when it involved children and he had a great way with them. I always find when visiting sick or disabled children that I feel I have to be very careful what I say but he could crack jokes and behave perfectly naturally without giving any offence.

There was, of course, another side to his character. He never missed an opportunity as I quickly discovered. I was approached by Gillette to appear in an advertisement and, as it was the first commercial deal I had been involved with, I thought I had better obtain permission and advice from my manager. I took the letter with me to show him and he told me to leave it with him and he would look into it. A week later he had sorted it all out but it was no longer just me but now Gordon Hill, Tommy Docherty and me. Doc, inevitably, was the star of the show and it was his car boot which was full of razors and blades rather than mine.

He was also fiercely competitive. One of our regular stopping-off places was Mottram Hall in Cheshire. We would stay there before big matches and when he was feeling particularly generous he would invite the wives to join us for a meal at Christmas or Easter. The restaurant was staffed mainly by Italians who were keen on soccer and quick to take advantage of the pitch in the grounds. Doc and Cav managed to get themselves involved in one of these games against a local side and, with a few drinks inside them and a vociferous audience from among the players, they turned the friendly into World War Two with abusive exchanges and tackles that were designed to snap oppenents in two. Doc was just as bad on tour abroad when, because of international calls, and an injury to Brian Greenhoff, he found himself on the substitutes' bench against Ajax in front of 100,000 people in Jakarta. His first tackle earned him a booking and he was fortunate that it was a friendly or he would surely have been sent off.

He was deliberately provocative off the pitch, often making comments tongue in cheek simply to get a reaction. Newspapermen have found him one of the most quotable managers in the game with no one safe from his sharp wit. Directors, in particular, were a target for his invective and while he was at United he said: 'The ideal Board of Directors should be made up of seven men – six dead and one dying.' Aston Villa Chairman Doug Ellis also felt Doc's biting tongue when he stated publicly that he was right behind the Doc who quipped back: 'I would sooner have him in front of me where I can see him.' The serious side would also come through as well, such as the time he observed: 'There's a hell of a lot of politics in football. I don't think Henry Kissinger would have lasted 48 hours at Old Trafford.' And: 'It's a rat race – the rats are winning.' But in the main his remarks were funny and clever. He was a genuinely amusing man who was happiest when he was in the spotlight and the bigger the stage the better. He needed a club like United, Manchester City, Arsenal or Spurs. I liked the man and still do. The Doc was always good medicine for me.

8

Dave Sexton

Tommy Docherty and Manchester United finally parted company on 3 July and instantly the names of the likely candidates for one of the most prestigious jobs in world football were eagerly discussed. The main contenders were eventually whittled down to three giants of the managerial world, Lawrie McMenemy, Brian Clough and Dave Sexton. Because it was close season there were none of the usual dressing room debates as to who was the right or wrong man for the job and though we all held our own personal opinions, we kept them to ourselves. My own feeling then as now is that Southampton's McMenemy would have fitted the bill.

There is something about McMenemy that makes him ideally suited to a big club like Manchester United and though he can be proud of what he has achieved with a comparatively small club like Southampton I am sure that he must now regret not having had a shot at one of the really big clubs while still a young man. You have to admire what he has done at the Dell over the years on a limited budget. He has continually achieved good results through remoulding and reshaping his sides as required. He has had his rows and difficulties with a variety of top players, all of which have been well publicised. To some this may make him a bad manager but I believe it happened because he has always been prepared to take on the problem players, of the sort that other managers are not prepared to stand up to. He has succeeded by harnessing that rebellious streak and turning it to the best advantage. Peter Osgood, Charlie George, Alan Ball, Frank Worthington, Mark Dennis . . . you can go on, the list is endless but they all responded to the big fellow. He also showed that he could compete with the big clubs and sign the players they all wanted and none was more notable than my England colleagues Kevin Keegan and Peter Shilton. If he could do that on a shoestring what could he have done with the sort of crowds and money that Manchester United have at their disposal?

Another of McMenemy's great assets is the way he handles the media. That may not be important with many clubs but with Manchester United it is an essential qualification and McMenemy seems to relish it.

Exactly the same applies to the controversial Brian Clough, though that was one appointment I could not see occurring, even if Brian Clough had wanted the job. Had he been following anyone else but the Doc then maybe there would have been a chance but, after the scandal surrounding Tommy's love affair, how could the Board possibly employ a man who was certain to rock the boat at some stage or another? He regularly criticises his directors and sometimes treats them with total contempt. This is the man who is reported to have said 'Football hooligans? Well, there are 92 chairmen for a start.' I doubt whether the Old Trafford directors could have coped with that sort of comment so soon after the turmoil of Doc's departure.

Having said that, what Clough has done in football is nothing short of miraculous. Like McMenemy he has proved himself by gaining results with less fashionable clubs; he has lifted them from nowhere to win League Championships and European Cups. Directors of clubs such as Derby and Forest can put up with the things he says and does because they know that the chances of finding someone who is even half as talented are remote in the extreme. He has insulted a succession of Forest chairmen but, with 18 months of his contract remaining and the promise of retirement at 50, they responded by giving him a presentation inscribed to 'Ten Glorious Years', and told him to write his own contract for as long as he liked. Could he have succeeded at a big club like United? Of course. The question mark was not over his ability to manage but how he would have survived boardroom battles. The bigger the club the more strongly it contests a manager's decisions. He is a man who needs to be boss – the sole boss. You take Clough as he is, warts and all, or not at all.

However, as the days progressed it became more and more obvious that the job would be given to Dave Sexton. They had even tried to appoint him seven years earlier as the successor to the ill-starred Wilf McGuinness but he had refused then because he felt he had a loyalty to Chelsea, whom he had just steered to FA Cup triumph. This time, however, he was available as he had been released by Queen's Park

Rangers – whom he had taken to within a whisker of the First Division Championship in 1976 – on the very day that Tommy Cavanagh had signed a long-term contract with the club, so severing any further possible ties with Tommy Docherty at Derby.

On the same day it was suggested in the papers that Sexton was about to sign as coach for Arsenal he became the new manager of Manchester United. The omens were good when he said: 'I want to see the team winning and playing attractive football. Which comes first? It must be winning. I've got to be honest and say that the image of Manchester United overawed me but this job must be the peak of ambition for any manager.' As far as I was concerned at the time it was the correct decision and not, as some people thought, because he was the antithesis of Tommy Docherty. Over the past few seasons we had been more enthusiastic than well prepared, and Dave came to us with a reputation for being an organisational coach with a flair for dreaming up terrific deadball kicks. Everyone told me he was quiet – and he was. My pre-season excitement was not lessened but increased with the change of manager, for I thought we would retain what we had already achieved because of Cav staying and that the arrival of Dave Sexton would add some ingredient we did not possess before.

That we did not win the title in Sexton's first season was blamed on the manager, as it usually is, but given we had the same players that we had before he joined, why didn't we? The answer can only be that it was down to the players themselves who failed to fulfil their potential.

Dave Sexton was very introspective and at the same time kind and generous. He hit exactly the right note when he arrived by making the point that he was taking over a talented, successful side and saw no point in changing the status quo. 'Let's keep it successful,' he said. 'Let's keep the ship going.' He was as good as his word, standing back to let Cav take those pre-season sessions and carry on with the sort of fitness training we had done in previous seasons. The only change he made was to whisk us away for a spell at a West German sports centre that he had used previously with Queen's Park Rangers.

It has to be stated that he was totally accepted in the dressing room in those early days whatever is said now. The players were extremely responsive, perhaps even more than they had been with Tommy. While the Doc did things his way, accepting no argument, Dave was always prepared to listen to the opinions of his senior players and act on their comments if he thought them justified. He was perfectly willing to change his mind for the good of the team whereas the Doc would only become angry if someone disagreed with him. There must be room for both types although ultimately the only things that matter in professional football are results.

Having worked under him, I must say that when it was announced in 1984 that he was to oversee the Football Association's project of training the cream of the country's young players at a live-in school at Lilleshall I felt that the job could well have been created for Dave. He always seemed to be more at ease with the younger players at United rather than with the established professionals. He introduced a lot of training routines designed to practise various elements of the game. He was a great technician and he wanted the players to do certain things a certain way. He even had a huge library of videos that he would use to illustrate his point and which would show the great players heading, shooting, tackling, crossing and so on. His training routines would incorporate practising these basic skills and concentrate on trying to improve technique. But how can you teach Martin Buchan to tackle, Gordon McQueen to head the ball or Jimmy Greenhoff to score goals? We could see what he was trying to achieve and would try and improve for him but you could see how much better his coaching worked with the younger players.

I suppose I have to come to the conclusion that, despite my deep respect for him and my initial excitement at his arrival, he was not the right manager for Manchester United. Perhaps it would have been very different if he had been coach or number two to a man like Lawrie McMenemy, then he could have left the administrative side of managing to someone else. Certainly he never hit it off with the Manchester Press. United has a unique rapport with the Press; the latter are in constant contact with the club and every national paper has a reporter who is in touch with the club every day. In this respect Manchester can be compared only with London but in many ways it is much worse because there is just United and City to occupy the local journalists' attention while in the capital there are any number of clubs to look to for a story. In London a manager can keep a low profile but in Manchester there is no hiding place as so many managers have discovered.

Dave never tried to be anything other than himself. He refused to put on a special face for the media. As a result he felt uncomfortable under their scrutiny. He also had that problem of taking over when the club were on a high after just winning the FA Cup. It wasn't just me who kept saying we could win the League, it was almost the entire team, the Press and half the city of Manchester.

Dave Sexton had no opportunity to ease himself into the job for even in the pre-season games there was crowd trouble which reflected badly on the club. The season proper opened with a repeat of the FA Cup Final with United, as Cup winners, playing the League and European Champions Liverpool, and Kenny Dalglish making his début. Instead of the glorious opening match it had promised to be the game was dull and ended in a goalless draw. We held our own but it was all a bit false and had very little to do with the season that was to follow.

Even so we had returned to action with a trophy in the cupboard, the sun on our backs and feeling on top of the world. We knew a little sparkle and spontaneity would be missing but to counterbalance that we did not expect to give away so much. It looked as though we had summed up our game well when we opened our League campaign with a thundering 4–1 victory at Birmingham City with Lou Macari scoring a hat-trick. We had no doubts and were on our way to the title.

The fans agreed, or at least the 57,000 who turned up at Old Trafford to see us beat Coventry City 2-1 did. Not even a 3-1 defeat in the local derby by Manchester City could weaken our resolve because, we told ourselves, anything can happen in those games and usually does, with the bottom teams beating the top ones and form going out of the window. But then we lost at home to Chelsea even though we did everything but score. This, sadly, was to prove typical. We beat Liverpool by two clear goals to go fifth but then lost to Middlesbrough and found ourselves in the middle of the table.

We were a model of inconsistency, beating Everton 6–2 at Goodison for their first defeat since August and then losing four games on the run. Typical of footballers we looked to Dave to do something about it even though we were puzzled and could offer no explanation as to why the same team that had promised so much was now achieving so little. The manager certainly tried to do his best for he went out and spent £800,000 buying first Joe Jordan and then Gordon McQueen from Leeds United.

My season was as mixed as the team's. I started quite well and enjoyed the change of position from wing to centre forward when Pancho Pearson was injured. People were surprised when I scored a few goals and that I had fitted in quite well but it was a role I had played at Tranmere while, under Doc, I had often been told to switch for ten minutes with Pancho to give him a break and me a change of scenery. It was all good publicity and a campaign to include me in the national team began in the Press. By November I had returned to the right wing, my form had dipped and I was picked for my first cap against Italy in a World Cup qualifying tie along with Peter Barnes and Bob Latchford – the latter had just ended a season in which he had bagged 30 goals. I was slightly worried because of my form and my experiences with Juventus but at least there was no chance of either Peter Barnes or I becoming conceited for, after the more formal greetings were over, manager Ron Greenwood told us, tongue-in-cheek, that he had had to select us because of all the media coverage we had been receiving. Yes, it was that sort of a season.

There was not even any respite for us in the Cup competitions. Trying for our third successive appearance in the FA Cup Final we went out to meet our jinx team, West Bromwich Albion. This time there was no pioneering spirit. We were the team to be shot down and rather than being the hungry team we had been before, we were everyone's target. To be frank we had been lucky to get past the first hurdle when we drew 1–1 with Carlisle and Brian Greenhoff was sent off. We beat them 4–2 in the replay and then drew Albion at Old Trafford. Footballers are notoriously superstitious and it is undoubtedly true that teams are affected by a run of losing to a particular opponent. Look at Spurs who went 73 years without a win against Liverpool at Anfield until last season; they were a goal down before they even started! Sure enough we went a goal down and it needed a late goal a few minutes from time by me to give us a replay at the Hawthorns. Even the goal had an element of luck about it as I cut in, let fly and saw the ball rebound off a post, against the back of Tony Godden's head and into the net. When we took Albion into extra time in the replay we thought we had broken the jinx but Cyrille Regis took the Cup out of our hands with a late goal.

We had already been knocked out of the League Cup in the second round – our first match – 3–2 by Arsenal while the European Cup Winners' Cup simply underlined the inconsistencies and problems the team and Dave Sexton faced in that first season.

Back in our rightful place in Europe we made headlines around the world for all the wrong reasons. We drew with the talented French side and former European Cup finalists, St Etienne, in the first round in France but this outstanding result was overlooked because of crowd trouble. Many of our supporters were injured and arrested as violence erupted on the terraces before the game. Once again it was the British who received the blame. The newspapers were full of it and the St Etienne President, Roger Rocher, delivered a bitter attack on our supporters, advised his own fans not to travel to the return match and lodged a protest with the European ruling body UEFA. Our Chairman Louis Edwards responded, claiming that non-segregation of fans was at fault while a Manchester police sergeant, at the game as a supporter, publicly accused the French police.

Undoubtedly drunkenness was a prime cause but all the precautions we now take for granted in this sort of match were totally ignored. Ours were working-class supporters going to a ground in an industrial town where they were allowed to stand in the middle of equally exuberant fans in the same area behind the goal. It was dynamite and no wonder there was an explosion. The violence seemed to die down once the game was under way and we felt very comfortable and fancied our chances in the return – until the unthinkable happened.

Manchester United, former European Champions and British pioneers in Europe, were banned from the Cup Winners' Cup. We were flabbergasted and our skipper Martin Buchan spoke for all of us when he said: 'We feel this decision is unjust because surely it should be the home club who are responsible for crowd control', while a disappointed Dave Sexton added: 'It seems a fantastic situation when the behaviour of the club and players is immaculate and yet both have to suffer.'

It would be wrong to suggest, however, that Manchester United, or in this case their fans, were totally innocent. Hooliganism had long been a problem for the club going back to 1969 when the club had been ordered to build a fence behind the Stretford End after the AC Milan goalkeeper had been felled in a barrage of missiles. Two years later the Football Association had stepped in and closed down the ground for two weeks following a knife-throwing incident and, worst of all, a derby match against City had had to be abandoned in 1974 when supporters invaded the pitch. Manchester City were awarded both points and the Football Association went a step further than the European ruling authority when it ordered the fans to be caged in with an eight-foot high fence.

However, until the St Etienne incident the record had been pretty good with virtually no trouble at Old Trafford and much better crowd control away, even though there had been problems at a pre-season friendly. We were amazed that the media should welcome the ban as the right course of action as we felt it had nothing to do with us. Indeed, the players had worked hard to ease the situation during my first season at the club by meeting and talking to the fans on Sunday mornings at Old Trafford; disassociating themselves from the hooligan element and setting an example with their own good behaviour on the pitch, which won two Fair Play awards in successive seasons.

Fortunately the club decided to appeal against the decision and headed their delegation with none other than Sir Matt Busby. I am sure that this well-respected figure had a great deal to do with our readmittance to UEFA when he said that the incident had not been 'intentional' and that it was recognised that the players' behaviour had been impeccable. The club were fined £7500 and ordered to play the second leg at least 300 kilometres from Old Trafford. It was a great relief, particularly as two days before the decision 54 fans were arrested at a League match with Leeds United. The fans were there for the taking that day, especially as the rivalry between Leeds and United supporters was enormous. We had beaten them in the semi-final of the Cup the year before and Leeds were beginning to slip from their lofty perch. But, even so, it prompted a decision from the club not to sell tickets for away matches. Surprisingly, former first-class referee, and the then Minister for Sport, Dennis Howell intervened on behalf of the fans.

One of the problems United face in controlling their supporters is that they come from all over the country. United has a cult following which has grown since the Munich air disaster. God knows football needs its supporters right now, but not the sort that attend matches for what happens off the pitch rather than on it.

Fortunately, only the right sort turned up at Home Park, Plymouth, when we played the return leg against the French team. But far from being the expected easy ride, the tie was now up in the air. It turned out to be a terribly emotional night with supporters attending to see wronged United and they not only closed the gates at Plymouth but there were also 30,000 people watching the game on a giant video screen at Old Trafford. What is more Plymouth provided us with a magnificent playing surface and we responded with a fine two-goal victory.

It was typical of that season that we should go into the next round and lose 4–0 to FC Porto in Portugal. But behind that result was an odd tale. We were due to play in Tehran a week later against the Iranian National team as part of the British Empire Exhibition. It meant that, after our game against Newcastle the previous Saturday, we had to have some of those vaccinations which cause a feverish reaction. When we played Porto on the Wednesday we all felt pretty rough and neither Jimmy Greenhoff nor David McCreery were able to play. We were playing far below our best and a Brazilian named Duda was quick to take advantage with a superb hat-trick.

Now Europe, to any team, means money and no club would jeopardise their chances by accepting a meaningless friendly so close to an important game no matter what the rewards. It is my belief that our reinstatement had been political. Had the British Government intervened in our European crisis and helped us back into the competition? Was this the price we had to pay and if so it was a very high price indeed. I believe we proved that we were the better side in the return at Old Trafford when, on another passionate night of European football, I scored twice as the team netted five goals. The only problem was that Porto broke away to score twice and win through to the third round on a slender 6–5 aggregate.

We finished that season in tenth place and, combined with our poor results in Europe, it represented a shocking season. It was reflected in our attitude both on the pitch and in the dressing room. We were not as resilient, that naivety had gone and, increasingly, the players began to look after themselves instead of each other. It would have been easy to blame the manager but the fault was the players' that season.

It brought about changes and, apart from the expensive newcomers, others were on their way out, one of them being my wing partner Gordon Hill. Tommy Docherty had been prepared to put up with Gordon's failings and eccentric behaviour in return for his 15 or so goals a season but Dave Sexton, and it must be said the players as well, were not. This must have become abundantly clear to the public when Martin Buchan was seen clipping him around the ear like a naughty schoolboy during a game. Gordon was a brilliantly instinctive player who enjoyed the match situation where he would often produce the unexpected and score outstanding goals. But if he was given specific instructions during a training session he would struggle. He was also encouraged to help out more in defence, particularly when we were going through a sticky patch, but he would get himself into all sorts of trouble as he tried to dribble his way out of the danger zone on the edge of our penalty area because it was alien to him just to boot the ball clear.

Gordon was a brash young cockney who had the habit of rubbing people up the wrong way when he spoke his mind. He was apt to put his foot in it – but still you could not help but like him. When he left, going to Derby County for £250,000 to rejoin Tommy Docherty, he claimed that there had been a vendetta against him in the dressing room but this was simply not true. We all recognised that he was a very gifted footballer and even in the season when things were going badly he scored 17 goals (7 of which were from the penalty spot) and we all felt sad that his skills could not be harnessed when necessary.

The dressing room atmosphere was certainly better without Gordon when we returned for the next season determined to put things right and win something. It was all bread and butter stuff, however, as there was not the glamour of Europe to liven up the domestic season and we had to watch with envy as Liverpool and the others enjoyed the limelight on that particular stage.

It was United's centenary year which made it doubly important that we should do well and put the previous season's disappointments behind us. The season looked promising when we began the celebrations by thrashing Real Madrid 4–0 in a friendly at Old Trafford and then opening our League challenge with two victories, beating Birmingham at home and Leeds away. But then we lost one and drew four of the next five to slip down the table to open a gap we could never close. Worse still we went out of the League Cup in disastrous fashion.

We were extremely fortunate to survive the opening round against our minnow neighbours Stockport County for, with barely five minutes to play, Gordon McQueen was sent off to leave us ten men and trailing 2 goals to 1. Stockport, on the verge of a great victory, lost their concentration and allowed our depleted team back into the game while goals from Sammy McIlroy and a Jimmy Greenhoff penalty in the last three minutes saw us through. But there was no escape in the next round when we were chased out of the competition by Third Division Watford with the young and then unknown striker Luther Blissett astonishing the Old Trafford crowd by scoring both the goals in the 2–1 victory.

We hovered between sixth and halfway positions in the League as Dave Sexton sought to find the winning combination. Goalkeeper Alex Stepney had been dropped and replaced by Paddy Roche. He was an unlucky goalkeeper for each time he made a mistake it was shown on television, with the replay being shown on the highlights for weeks until he made his next error. Goalkeepers are always likely to make mistakes early on in their careers and most overcome it but the media destroyed any hopes this young man had of making a career at Old Trafford.

Sexton tried to buy Scottish international Jim Blyth from Coventry City but the deal fell through on medical grounds and as a result a young man, Gary Bailey, was given his chance. This striking youth with blond hair and a South African accent had suddenly appeared from nowhere. The first I had seen of him had been while I was working on a television film with Gordon Hill the season before. The filming required someone to stand between the sticks while Gordon and I pumped goals past them for the cameras. The problem was that this young unknown kept stopping them. Gary was keen and worked terrifically hard at improving his game even though he was another who was apt to speak his mind and upset one or two people on the way. He came into the side for his first game on a wet day against Ipswich Town and did enough to keep his place for the rest of the season. Admittedly he made his share of mistakes but he never allowed it to shake his confidence and I believe he will go on to earn a great many England caps.

Another newcomer was Welshman Micky Thomas who came into the side a couple of games later. He was a non-stop worker who could have stayed with United for a long time if he had wanted. He was hard to fathom, a strange young man who used to travel to Manchester every day from his home in Wales. He was not the brightest of people, on his own admission, and became a target for the biting humour of Lou Macari who would pursue him everywhere until one day Micky went missing. We found him hiding from his tormentor in the sauna.

My own form was pretty good for I had grown in confidence and reputation by becoming a regular in the England squad. I was an automatic choice at United and, coming up to my twenty-fourth birthday, I felt that I was approaching my peak. Indeed I finished that season without having missed a match (one of four successive seasons) and as top scorer, along with Jimmy Greenhoff, with eleven goals.

Although our form was dreadfully inconsistent we were still capable of beating anyone on our day and it was with this attitude that we embarked on our Cup campaign, the last thing left open to us that season. The preparations were hardly the best as the season was gripped in an icy spell that saw only three ties survive the freeze on the day of the third round while we failed to play a single League game during the month of January. We were paired with Chelsea at Old Trafford and though they were a poor side and were to be relegated at the end of the season, the game was a lottery on that frozen pitch. We won 3–0 in a game which was notable for me as I scored a rare headed goal. But it was hardly take-off time as we limped through the next round against Fulham by a single goal after a draw at Craven Cottage while we were distinctly lucky to win our fifth round tie with a Jimmy Greenhoff goal at Third Division Colchester after Martin Buchan had cleared off the line. We were riding our luck again and those old sayings of Tommy Docherty's came tumbling back – could we make it to Wembley for the third time in four years?

The sixth round draw, away to Tottenham, however, suggested otherwise and when we went a goal down to the Argentinian World

Cup star Ossie Ardiles, it looked as though our season was going to come to an end then and there at White Hart Lane. Luckily Micky Thomas chose that game to score his first goal for the club and we took Spurs back to Old Trafford where we saw them off with goals from Joe Jordan and Sammy McIlroy. Again we were one game away from Wembley.

Once more we found ourselves face to face with our old rivals Liverpool, at the time looking within easy grasp of yet another Championship, at Maine Road. Although it was handy for our fans we would have preferred to meet them at our old stamping ground, Hillsborough. It was a game with so many twists and turns that the outcome was in doubt until the end. Kenny Dalglish put Liverpool ahead with a good goal only for Joe Jordan to take advantage of a Ray Clemence mistake to equalise. We then felt we had the match sewn up when, after Terry McDermott had missed a penalty, Brian Greenhoff put us ahead with a looping volley.

All we had to do was hold out until the end but with only six minutes remaining we were shattered when Alan Hansen broke through to grab an equaliser. Liverpool had played badly and survived and, understandably, they were convinced they would see us off in the replay at Goodison Park. In contrast we were shattered at having come so close and then allowing it to slip and I, personally, felt deeply despondent. The next day we were supposed to play in a professional footballers' golf tournament and while the Liverpool players were there in force, we were represented by one player. But football is nothing if not unpredictable and on Liverpool's home ground we beat them with a single Jimmy Greenhoff goal and there we were back at our Wembley home yet again ready to face Arsenal who had beaten Wolves by two clear goals at Villa Park.

We had been through this before and though Dave Sexton was a different personality from the effervescent Tommy Docherty, the build-up was similar even to the extent of staying at the same hotel, the Selsdon Park in Surrey. My room-mate was, once again, my mate Brian Greenhoff who was apt to suffer pre-match nerves before big games. He had survived the previous finals without too many problems but this one was different. Maybe it was because Brian had not been a regular in the side that season and was not even certain he was in the team to face Arsenal, though it was more likely than not. The night before the final he had a violent attack of nerves for he had never learned to live with them and, in the early hours of Saturday morning he was in and out of bed, running to the toilet and complaining of stomach pains. He tried his best to keep quiet but switching on the light had woken me up and, naturally, I was concerned about him.

He couldn't get back to sleep and when he wasn't shuttling back and forth from the bathroom he was playing Cribbage with himself. It was not ideal preparation for either of us but he was my best pal, and I knew that if I telephoned one of the staff to ask for another room Brian's chances of playing would drop to zero. In the end Brian convinced himself that he was so ill he called Laurie Brown for help. His chances of playing went with that call, though I still believe to this day that Brian could and should have played.

The first 20 minutes of a game, particularly a Wembley final, are always crucial and Arsenal, with Liam Brady playing brilliantly, threatened to take us apart. As it was he sparked off a move that created a goal for Brian Talbot and then, minutes before the half-time interval, he laid on a chance for Frank Stapleton, later to become a United player, to score the second. After that the game drifted away from us, and though we tried hard, we could not get back into it. Pat Jennings tipped a shot from Macari over the bar and comfortably held another effort from mc. Arsenal were already celebrating their victory on the bench when they sent on the fresh legs of Steve Walford for David Price.

Suddenly it all changed with an explosion of goals which turned an ordinary Cup Final into a memorable one, the like of which had not been seen since Sir Stanley Matthews inspired Blackpool to their 4–3 victory over Preston North End back in 1953. Gordon McQueen, never one to allow his head to drop, stuck out a foot from a corner to deflect the ball past Pat Jennings with 86 minutes 20 seconds of the game gone. It breathed new life into us and panic began to spread through the previously confident Arsenal side and slightly less than two minutes later we were level when Sammy McIlroy twinkled his way through the retreating defenders to score.

At that moment my imagination ran riot. We were heading for extra time and a lost game had been saved. I was so convinced that we were going to win that I could even see the headlines in the Sunday papers.

The score would be 4–2. It was inevitable, we were tall and strong, full of running and they were shattered at having come so close, only to lose it. All we had to do was keep at it for 100 seconds.

We failed. The game was in its last 50 seconds when Liam Brady once more came striding forward, feeding Graham Rix on the left to cross for Alan Sunderland who forced the ball past Gary Bailey with scarcely enough time left for us to restart the game. I have never switched from feeling elated to deflated so quickly. A lot of people blamed Gary Bailey for the goal but you could start criticising long before the ball reached him. We should have killed it, fouled or anything at that stage.

Our manager Dave Sexton blamed the defeat on our lack of concentration and described it as a cruel result. It was as cruel for him as it was for us as it left him with nothing to show for his hard work and his expenditure, with not even a place in Europe. He must have spent the summer considering what changes he needed to make for United to become a successful team. One strong possibility was that Sexton would return to Stamford Bridge to sign Ray Wilkins. Ray had first joined him as a 12-year-old associate schoolboy before being signed as an apprentice three years later.

I had become friendly with Ray at England get-togethers and as we said goodbye after England's close season tour to Bulgaria, Sweden and Austria I had said I would see him at pre-season training. He had just smiled but, a few weeks later, he signed for a staggering £825,000 and Sexton admitted he had been chasing him ever since our Cup Final defeat. The manager financed the deal by selling: Stuart Pearson to West Ham for £220,000; David McCreery to Derby for £200,000; and my old mate Brian Greenhoff to Leeds United for £350,000. Whatever anyone thought of the players who went they had to admit that it was very good business. The timing of the sales was good and he achieved the maximum return when any sort of delay could have reduced the fee. None of the three was as successful once they left United.

Until this season Sexton had always been in charge of someone else's team and had been judged on players who were not his. No matter how well players perform under one manager it does not mean that they will fit in with new ideas and a new manager. At last Sexton's side was taking shape and he was immediately repaid with a good solid start inspired in no small way by the play making of Ray Wilkins. The great irony, if dressing room talk can be believed, was that the one player whom Sexton wanted to complete his line up was Bryan Robson, later to become the United captain and a major playing influence on the team. The gossip went that the Board would not release the money that Dave Sexton needed to complete his signing.

Even without Robson we were top by early October, and for once were the bystanders while other teams had problems. Brighton's goal-keeper Eric Steele and Gary Williams were cautioned for scuffling with each other as we won 2–0 and went to the top. We were playing the way Dave Sexton hoped we would and though we were playing some very good matches, our style was not exactly in United's tradition. It was more the sort of considered football that QPR used to play under Sexton's rule than the smash and grab of Docherty.

Gradually, together with Liverpool, we moved ahead of the pack and, very soon, it became evident that it was going to be a two-horse race. But while Liverpool had their usual cutting edge and streak of ruthlessness, we again lacked consistency. We were capable of beating Liverpool one week and losing to Wolves the next. Dave Sexton often used to talk to us about the perfect performance, being 3 up at half-time and going on to win 6–0. We came close to it with a marvellous display against Norwich where we fell a goal short in a match described as superb by both managers.

The perfect performance finally came at Ipswich – the only problem being that we were on the receiving end as Paul Mariner scored a hat trick and Alan Brazil (another player eventually to join United) two. Gary Bailey spared us from being totally humiliated with two penalty saves. We changed our game that day with Martin Buchan doing a man-for-man on Eric Gates who dragged him all over the park and left gaping holes for the rest of the Ipswich team to exploit.

That match summed up the sort of season we had had. Norwich, who we beat twice in the League by scoring seven times without reply, beat us 4–1 in the League Cup after we had beaten Spurs 4–3 on aggregate in a two-legged match. By a remarkable coincidence we drew Tottenham again in the third round of the FA Cup and looked like repeating our early success when we held them to a 1–1 draw at White Hart Lane. We were odds-on certainties when goalkeeper

Aleksic was carried off after a clash with Joe Jordan and Glenn Hoddle took over in goal. Joe was a fearsome sight when in full cry but I do not believe that he deliberately intended to hurt anyone but only to frighten them. This was a 50–50 clash but Joe had to shoulder the usual blame.

We thought we had only to turn out in the second half to win the game but we could not get back into our rhythm and Spurs had taken us into extra time when Ossie Ardiles picked up the ball just inside our penalty area and hit a screaming shot into the top corner. I was standing next to him and could only admire the shot and the goal. To make things worse it was our first home defeat of the season.

We were left with only the League to concentrate on. We clawed back a six-point gap and drew level on 26 April when we beat Coventry City while Liverpool drew with Crystal Palace. But even though we came close we were, in all honesty, just behind them all the way and we should at least have put pressure on them by beating Leeds in our last game while the Merseysiders were crushing Aston Villa 4–1. The odd thing was that Dave Sexton used to set targets for us, such as a number of goals for individual players. He said that to win the Championship we needed to win 25 games and draw 10. Liverpool did exactly that while we won 24 and lost 8!

During the season United suffered a tragic loss when Chairman Louis Edwards died of a heart attack. It came just a month after a *World in Action* investigative programme by the northern-based Granada television company had probed into his business affairs, alleging slush funds and irregular dealings on the stock market. I did not know anything about that side of his business, but I did like him. He was a large, genial character who loved Manchester United and was the soul of the place. His infectious laughter could often be heard as you walked into the club and you always felt in good spirits in his company. To me the television programme had seemed especially vindictive from a company that we had to deal regularly with. I know it had a profound effect on Louis and his son Martin, now Chairman of the club, is certain that it helped bring on his premature death.

I don't know enough of how the Stock Exchange works to understand the ethics of Louis Edwards' dealings but what I found particularly abhorrent was the way the television company tapped his telephone calls. I thought it was more like the treatment a suspected terrorist might receive. It might have made good viewing but to launch a campaign against a man like that was, to me, very wrong. There was no smirking in the dressing room next morning, everyone was sorry for Edwards and how he had been portrayed by a programme that had robbed him of all dignity.

Edwards had become a member of the Old Trafford Board of Directors the day after the Munich air disaster and, from then on, had worked hard for the club. Inevitably over that number of years he was certain to make a few enemies no matter how well he was liked. The television programme made full use of those people.

It may also have had an effect on the future of Dave Sexton for there is no doubt that Louis Edwards liked him and may well have supported him when it came to the crisis point – and that was to come all too quickly.

Dave Sexton was subjected to ridiculous pressures that season. He knew that he desperately needed to win something though he knew he was on the right lines having finished a close second to Liverpool even if it was not a typical Manchester United side. Neither, at the start, was it a Dave Sexton side for the nucleus of his team were all missing in the opening games of the season with: Joe Jordan hurt in the first match – a 3–0 win over Middlesbrough – which put him out for 7 games, Gordon McQueen and, most important of all, playmaker Ray Wilkins, both having just 11 games each towards the end of the season.

Although we lost only one of our next eleven matches – we won just two. That was the pattern of the season, bankers on the pools coupons. The best we achieved in the League was fourth place but, in the main, we stayed mid-table and finished a disappointing eighth, losing only one but drawing eleven of our home games and seven away. There was no solace to be gained in the cup competitions either, as we went out at the first try to Coventry City who deservedly beat us 1–0 home and away. The same fate awaited us in the UEFA Cup when the Poles of Widzew Lodz held us 1–1 at home and then survived a good United display on their own ground, including a Coppell shot which hit the post, to go through on away goals in a 0–0 draw.

Not even our favourite FA Cup could save us this time. We pulled back from two goals down at Old Trafford to yet another draw against

Brighton and beat them 2–0 away. We then fell foul of Brian Clough and his Nottingham Forest side. Long before then the knives were drawn out for Dave Sexton with a campaign in the newspapers for his dismissal with three of the senior Manchester football writers, nicknamed the 'Gang of Three' at Old Trafford, saying openly that he should go in their newspapers and on television.

It did not help that Dave Sexton's most expensive acquisition, Garry Birtles from Nottingham Forest, failed to live up to the over-the-top price tag of £1,250,000. It was incredible money even at a time when transfer fees were going crazy. Trevor Francis broke the £1 million barrier and, to my mind, was worth it, but once that psychological barrier had been overcome there was some very silly money flying about football and many clubs were to carry the legacy into the eighties. United, wealthier than most due to their large gates, have been able to indulge their managers' whims and go to limits and, in Garry's case, they backed Dave.

Garry, an England international, had been an outstanding player with Forest but he could not find scoring form for United. He scored one all season and that was in the Cup tie. Garry used to make a point of saying how much he would prefer to be laying carpets (his previous job) and having a pint and a laugh with his mates in a local pub. He never really settled in at Manchester and even after he moved house he would race back to the Midlands at every opportunity to play one of his mates at squash. He did not get on at all with the local journalists but liked the fans who were very fair to him. He and Joe Jordan were never a pair, wherein lay much of the problem.

Nikolai Jovanovic, one of Yugoslavia's most talented players who had joined us from Red Star the previous season for £300,000, also found it difficult to settle in and we never saw the best of this six-foot tall footballer. He simply did not have the home bred players' passion for the daily grind of the League programme and he became disillusioned as he spent half the season in the reserves which was not what he had come to United for. My lasting memory of Niki is garlic! He changed next to me and I swear he must have eaten the vegetable sprinkled on his cornflakes. At least I always used to be the quickest to get changed.

Others, myself included, did not play well or consistently. It was our failure at home which brought the most pressure. Sides have always come to Old Trafford and tried to put up the shutters but this time we did not have the guile or the creative ability to break them down. At a club as big as Manchester United you can only be judged by results and it became a question of 'when' Dave would leave rather than 'if' and we were all surprised that he survived our Cup defeat at Forest.

It seemed, for a while, as if the directors were prepared to give him another chance when we won our last seven games of the season as injured players Wilkins and McQueen settled back into their stride but these factors probably only delayed the inevitable and Martin Edwards announced that the club were terminating Dave's contract at the end of the season. There were not many who could hold their heads up. I know I had a bad season. I came back from the European Championships in Italy to have a hernia operation and just had time to squeeze in two weeks holiday from the day I had my stitches out until we reported for pre-season training. I was tired and stale after five or six seasons without a break and it showed in my play.

At the end of every season the United players would walk around the pitch after the last home game for a lap of honour. It was a display of mutual admiration with the supporters applauding us and we in turn thanking them. That season I felt I was taking their cheers under false pretences. Maybe I was being hypercritical but at a time when I should have been playing my best football I did not live up to my expectations and this did not help the manager.

It was a sad day when Sexton went for we all liked his sincerity and his honesty. I am not the only United player who keeps in regular contact with him. Another era had come to an end at Old Trafford and within a few weeks Dave Sexton was manager of Coventry City and shortly afterwards Ron Atkinson was appointed manager of Manchester United.

9

A Clean Sweep with Ron Atkinson

Ron Atkinson became manager of Manchester United on 9 June 1981 putting at an end weeks of speculation as to who would succeed the departed Dave Sexton. Once again the name of Southampton manager Lawrie McMenemy had been tipped, so strongly in fact that I could not believe it when he turned the job down and I can assume only that he was not satisfied that he would enjoy the same sort of power he had at the Dell. Many other personalities were in the headlines as possibilities. Celtic put a veto on talks with Billy McNeill, Aston Villa's contentious manager Ron Saunders was supposed to have had talks with the club, while Bobby Robson was another name that was bandied about. In the end the job dropped into the lap of that colourful character, West Bromwich Albion boss Ron Atkinson. Fourth choice, outsider, call him what you like, he didn't need to be asked twice.

However, it was not as if the choice of Ron Atkinson had come out of the blue. His name had loomed large on the list of candidates, which was hardly surprising to anyone connected with United considering the sticky time West Bromwich had given us over recent years. He had developed a fine team and had achieved considerable results right from the grass roots of the Southern League with Kettering Town into the League with less than glamorous Cambridge United and then unfashionable West Bromwich. At times, he was loud, brash and appeared to go over the top. He was certainly big enough for the job.

I happened to be at Old Trafford a couple of days after Atkinson's arrival. He called me into his office for a quick chat which turned into a long discussion over several cups of tea. It was flattering but Ron was just showing his shrewdness for a number of senior players were given the same treatment as he picked the brains of everyone he could get hold of to develop some background information. He instantly struck me as a good talker but, like all footballers with a new manager, I was wary of him. Would he rate me highly? Did I figure in his plans? What lay ahead for all of us? He had obviously arrived at Old Trafford with great enthusiasm even though there had been much acrimony over his departure from the Hawthorns. I wondered if he would have been quite so sure of himself and the importance of the position had he witnessed our bizarre summer tour to Asia before his appointment.

I was not on this tour at the start as I was away enjoying somewhat mixed fortunes during England's World Cup qualifying games in Switzerland and Hungary. Having played in the disaster in Switzerland I was cock-a-hoop following our great come-back against Hungary and I telephoned the club to find out what arrangements had been made for Mick Duxbury, Gary Bailey and me when we returned from international duty. The United team had been left under the guidance of reserve team trainer Jack Crompton and physiotherapist Laurie Brown and even before they left Manchester on the tour both Sammy McIlroy and Jimmy Nichol had pulled out. Also the unpredictable Mick Thomas, encouraged by some of the other players, shocked the temporary management when he made his decision to leave at Heathrow, so late that his bags had already been loaded on the aircraft.

With others away on international duty and Ray Wilkins making it clear he had no intention of going straight from the England trip to Asia for a pointless tour, United were down to bare bones. So much so that they arrived in Kuala Lumpur for the first game with just 11 players. In order to make a reasonable impression, they roped in a young lad on the plane, who was on his way to visit his girlfriend, to act as a substitute. I met the lad in a bar later in the tour and, as a United fanatic, he was so delighted at this unexpected honour that he spent the entire match sprinting up and down the line, warming-up in case he was required.

Such were the problems that the tour organisers insisted on meeting Mick, Gary and me at Luton Airport on England's return from Buda- pest, escorting us to an hotel in the Heathrow complex and waiting with us for eight hours until we were due to fly out and join the party. It was almost like being under house arrest and, quite clearly, they did not want to risk any more walk-outs as the guarantee to the club revolved around the number of internationals present on the tour. Because of a bribes scandal in Singapore, the tour arrangements had already been altered several times and no sooner had we arrived than we were whisked off to Borneo for the next game. We found ourselves in a new oil-strike town which, like the old gold rush towns of the West, had grown somewhat quickly, and the quality of our hotel, the Shangri La, hardly reflected its name – it was anything but! In fact it was so bad that the players and directors decided to squat in the foyer, which doubled as a transport cafe, refusing to go to our rooms. It was a futile move because, in the end, there was simply nowhere else.

It was awful, as was the rest of the trip. We were told we would be playing against top sides but we found ourselves up against Mickey Mouse outfits. The legal wrangles that followed went on for years and, so far as I know, may still be. It was not very nice for any of us but I felt more than sorry for Jack Crompton who had been thrown in at the deep end because we had no manager. He said at the time that he didn't know why he should put up with all the aggravation when he was returning to a new manager and might find himself out of a job altogether when he came home. Those were prophetic words for Ron Atkinson sacked him and Laurie Brown in a clean sweep when he brought in all his own men from West Bromwich and other clubs.

Not that I was terribly concerned for I had my mind on more urgent and important matters. Unknown to anyone at the club I was planning to marry my childhood sweetheart Jane when I got back. I was not being a prima donna or anything like that, it was simply that for something as private as your own wedding I didn't want our pictures splashed across the Sunday papers. It had all come together gradually, beginning when I had bought a new house the previous September. We had been together a long time and it was only a question of when we would marry. We finally made up our minds in February but, because of my football commitments, we had to leave it until the end of the tours which meant Jane had to arrange everything. I was away for seven or eight weeks all told and even when I returned to England I stayed in London to go and see the pop group Pink Floyd on the Wednesday night and then to buy my ice blue wedding suit in London the next day. I went back to Manchester on the Thursday to buy a pair of pale blue shoes from my favourite shop.

From there I went straight to my parents in Liverpool and on the Sunday, the eve of the wedding, I went out for the traditional pint or two with my mates. When I got back I thought that I had better take my wedding clothes inside from the boot of my car and hang them up. On my way up to the bedroom I stopped and asked my Mum if she had ever seen a suit and shoes like these. She hadn't because when I took out my pale blue shoes to show her they were both left feet! The salesman could only have been a Manchester City fan with a very warped sense of humour.

What was I to do? There I was in Liverpool at midnight on Sunday, getting married at Northwhich in Cheshire 20 miles away and with my right shoe 25 miles in the opposite direction in Manchester. I started telephoning the shoe shop at 8 o'clock the next morning, getting a poor, bemused cleaning lady first before speaking to an apologetic manager at 9 a.m. Fortunately a friend was coming from that area and it was arranged that someone from the shop should meet him midway and hand over the vital shoe at Mere Golf Club, in the hope that my friend would arrive with it in time for the 11 a.m. wedding. I set off for my wedding wearing one pale blue shoe and one black one, with a pair of blue sneakers tucked under my arm just in case the unthinkable happened.

Halfway to the church I turned to my best man, who was my grandfather Eric, and asked him if he had everything, the rings and such like. 'What rings?' he asked. 'The ones I left out for you on the kitchen table,' I replied thinking he was winding me up. Unfortunately he wasn't and we screeched to a halt at the first telephone box only to find that everyone had already left home on the 20-mile drive to the church. Goodness knows what the vicar thought when I turned up in odd shoes to tell him I had forgotten the ring but matters improved when my mate arrived like Prince Charming with the missing shoe while Jane provided a substitute ring, an eternity ring I had given her a couple of years earlier. There was not a lot Jane could say about my mishaps for, that very morning, she had taken her wedding dress out of its wrapping to discover that the shop had given her the wrong dress with the one provided several sizes too large for my blushing bride.

How we kept the whole thing secret with so much going on I will never know but, sure enough, we arrived at the hotel in Hale for our reception which had been booked by Jane under her maiden name to be greeted by a surprised manager. He knew me because I had eaten there several times before. What a coincidence, he said, because only the day before Manchester City captain Paul Power had held his reception in the very same place. He should have kept his mouth shut for when we walked into the room for the meal all the tables were neatly laid with little posies of pale blue flowers – Manchester City's colours. It was rather obvious after what he had told us and my wife's mother, Eileen, was furious because she had paid for fresh flowers and was being fobbed off with some that had already been used.

What is it they say about something borrowed, something blue! At least we had a good laugh about it when we headed out for New York on the way to our honeymoon in Bermuda. I had told Jane how good television was in the United States and as soon as we arrived at the hotel I turned on the 'idiot's lantern' to prove my point and, to Jane's disgust, spent the next half hour watching *The Flintstones* while my bride waited patiently to go out for dinner.

Never mind, the dream was still to come. I knew that the hotel we were going to stay in at Bermuda was ideal because I had seen it while on a tour with United. It was one of those posh, colonial buildings ironically owned by Everton's top man John Moores. We checked in and the first thing I asked was what time was dinner in the restaurant as we were both famished. The large black receptionist told me that I would have time to change but I replied that we would just drop our bags and come straight down. 'But you need a tie, sir,' he said.

'I don't have one with me', I replied as it is not something a footballer usually takes with him on a trip.

'Ah!' he responded, 'if you tell us what sort of jacket you will be wearing we will provide sir with a tie.'

'I don't have a jacket, either,' I said, becoming extremely irritated, only to become more so when he went away to reappear with one of those bright red, two-button things a waiter might wear. I told him exactly what he could do with it and stormed off with Jane to eat in the coffee bar.

The problem was that this difficulty was going to arise again and again if we wanted to eat properly. We went into Hamilton and, out of principle, I refused to pay £300 for a jacket plus another £100 for the shirt and tie to go with it. Fortunately for Jane we met a family from Bolton and they had a well kitted-out son of my size who kindly lent me the necessary garments for the duration of our stay. After a day or two the guy who had caused me all the problems discovered that I was a footballer and spent the rest of our stay there trying to tell me he was Manchester United's greatest fan but it fell on deaf ears.

At least I arrived back in Manchester tanned and ready for the latest challenge. It was obvious from what Ron Atkinson had been saying to the newspapers that there were going to be changes, not that he had had much choice when Big Joe Jordan, at the end of his contract told him he was off to Italy to join AC Milan. The new manager made an immediate impression with his replacement for if you are going to replace a player of Jordan's quality who better than Frank Stapleton? He had caused the United defence enough trouble over the years for us to be thankful that he was going to be on our side.

It was good business which ever way you looked at it. Such were the spiralling transfer fees then that Arsenal rejected United's initial bid of £750,000 and put a price tag around his neck of £2 million. Ron, to his credit, instantly reduced his bid by £100,000. Eventually the arbitration committee valued Frank at £1.1 million including value added tax and all levies. But if United thought they had problems with that deal it was nothing compared with the animosity which grew between Ron and his old club.

Mick Brown and Brian Whitehouse had left the Hawthorns' coaching staff to link up with us at United and then our manager caused a stir by announcing that his targets were Albion skipper Bryan Robson and his fellow midfield player Remi Moses. There was a reported £2 million offer on the table to support the bid. Three days later Remi Moses joined the club he had supported as a youngster for £500,000, but Albion manager Ronnie Allen stated: 'Bryan Robson leaves over my dead body', while his Chairman Bert Millichip added: 'He is one player who is not available at any price'. Two weeks later Bryan Robson signed on the dotted line at Old Trafford in front of 46,837 witnesses before our 5–0 win over Wolves and not a corpse in sight. Everyone accepted the price paid for Stapleton but there were some doubts over the cost of the pair from West Bromwich Albion, and you could hear people asking whether or not they were worth it.

They were described as Atkinson's favourites and while Robson was an English international with a growing reputation, Remi was unknown. Even now Remi is seen by a great many people as simply a hard worker. You have to play and train with him to appreciate that he is a great deal more than that. He has brought grit and courage to the United midfield and he has shown his character by surviving some early sniping, emerging as one of the crowd's favourites. In terms of a Berti Vogt style of marking I cannot think of anyone better in the country. He has staying power and if he was told to stick close to someone like Platini he would not give him a touch. Remi is no one's fool and, what is more, he is still improving, as England manager Bobby Robson was quick to recognise when he included him in his World Cup qualifying squads in the 1984-85 season.

The arrival of Bryan Robson showed that every player has his price whatever his club may say and, of course, Ron Atkinson's judgement has been completely backed by events and Robson's stature in the world game. As for his price, United could have doubled their money if they had chosen to sell him to Sampdoria in Italy instead of Ray Wilkins to AC Milan.

Ron Atkinson had promised to bring top players to the club and he was living up to his word. Apart from those already mentioned, John Gidman, one of the game's great characters, joined us in an exchange deal with Everton for Mick Thomas while the names of Trevor Francis, Mark Lawrenson and Frank Worthington were also mentioned.

It was all heady stuff but it was passing me by a little for, after a basically injury-free run, I injured my ankle in a pre-season tournament in Aberdeen. I was getting excellent treatment from United's new physiotherapist Jim Headridge but, tragically, he collapsed and died during a training session only a few weeks after joining us. Football suffered a number of sad losses that year, only a few weeks later, my idol, the former Liverpool manager, Bill Shankly, passed away and then in November, 42-year-old England coach Bill Taylor died. All this was in the space of three months.

Our new manager had a number of injury problems in those first weeks of the season and though I was nowhere near fit I was a lot fitter than some of the others and, in my wisdom and enthusiasm, I decided to play. Obviously I wanted to impress Atkinson but I have to say now that neither he nor anyone else on the staff put me under any pressure to play. It was my own decision – and it was a bad one. I was rubbish in those first few weeks and, after only two points from our first four games, we were at the bottom of the First Division. Gradually our form began to improve and my injury began to mend, along with the others' who had been jostling for a place on the treatment table. There was also a certain Bryan Robson to fit in. Then, an hour and a half before the local derby against Manchester City, Ron Atkinson called me to one side and told me I was the one who was going to be left out to make way for our new signing. It was the first time I had been dropped and though the blow was somewhat softened by being made substitute I did not like it and told him so, adding that I would prove him wrong.

I had my chance then and there when Garry Birtles came off. I played terribly as we drew 0–0 at Maine Road. I was back in the side, however, with Sammy out for the next game against Birmingham City and I even scored in a 1–1 draw at Old Trafford but an interesting side effect of my being dropped was a sudden interest in my future by a number of clubs including West Ham United, Coventry City and Arsenal. Ron called me in and told me that he had had an offer and that his friend, John Bond at Manchester City, had advised him to accept. I told him thank you – but no thank you. I said that I had a contract and would see it out.

It did not, of course, end there. We played in a testimonial at Arsenal and rumours were rife that I was going to join West Ham for £1 million. Everyone assumed I would take the money and run, especially after being dropped and I surprised all of them by saying that I was not interested in the money I could make but only in honouring my contract. I supposed it harked back to Tommy Docherty's days when he told me that any move from Manchester United was a step down and at 26 years of age I was not ready to take that downward step. I am a pretty frugal person and feel that I have always worked hard for what I have got. But this time the £50,000 or £60,000 I could have picked up for such a move was not the most important factor.

Ron had sold players like Jimmy Nicholl and Sammy McIlroy to try and balance the books a little and no doubt my going would have helped in that respect too but he did not push the matter and, in fact, said that he would be happy if I stayed. There was no quarrel then or since. I have always got on with the big fellow and have never fallen out with him. Ron is an honest man with the courage of his convictions and he has my respect.

At the start of his first season he stood back slightly and took in what we had to offer before making his mark and bringing in new players. When we were bottom he went on television and laughed at the situation saying that, come May, we would be in there shouting with the best. He was right and within six weeks we had gone top with an unbeaten run of a dozen matches.

He is his own man and he does not think twice about making a difficult decision such as leaving out one of his senior players if he thinks it is right for his team. It might not seem so at the moment and, indeed, I felt slighted when he axed me, but I knew he was right when I reflected on my form before the game and, after all, it was up to me whether or not I played with an injury.

Ron had and still has in some quarters an image of being 'flash'. When too much was made of it in the Press he cut down on the gold trinkets dramatically. It is the same with his champagne drinking. Certainly Ron can drink with the best of them but, more often than not, he would have the same full glass in his hand while those around him had had their's filled half a dozen times. He was shrewd and knew when to drink and when not to. He would drink, for instance, with the players but never to the extent of getting drunk with them. He is a firm believer in the proverb, 'familiarity breeds contempt'. One thing he does like, however, are good cars, and it is reported that when he was discussing his car with the club before signing, Martin Edwards told him that Dave Sexton had a Rover. Ron replied that he had a dog named Charlie but he was talking about cars not dogs. He finished up with a Mercedes – champagne-coloured, of course.

Ron kept training as simple as possible. We practised crossing, shooting and playing in five-a-sides but were not given a great deal of coaching. He reckoned he had the best players around and that his job was to make sure they were fit after which it was up to them to prove their skills. One of the best parts of his management, to my mind, was his team talk. This has to be done 42 times a season before League games as well as before Cup matches. Ron always made his interesting with his off-the-cuff chat which helped put everyone in the right frame of mind. His main failing was that he was inflexible. Ron had his own way of dealing with things and that was it. An example was when I recovered my form and the club stepped in with the offer of a five-year contract which I thought was an enormous commitment for them to make. I discussed it with Ron and we agreed on everything except one minor point. It had nothing to do with more money, but just how it was to be paid. It made little difference to Ron but he kept to his ground and, in the end, said: 'Sod it, take it or leave it. You've got 24 hours to decide.' I asked him if he minded whether I talked about it to the Chairman. He said that was fine and within a very short time it was all settled.

I suppose there is a lot to be said for the Liverpool system where the manager has no responsibility for the contractual side of his players, leaving all of that to Peter Robinson, the Chief Executive, and to the Chairman John Smith. If I was a coach or manager at Liverpool I would, at the least, want to sit in on the discussions, but then that is the side of management which attracts me.

Martin Edwards was to add the title of Chief Executive to that of Chairman during that season though there are some eyebrows raised at the money he takes out of the club. Why not? A Chairman, whether it be a large company or a football club, takes a fat salary for making important decisions and taking responsibility, not for the hours he puts in. As Chairman of Manchester United, spending so much money on players and entertaining so many spectators, he has a great responsibility – though I am still amazed that he bought a basketball team.

After that bad start we lost only five more League games but, once again, had to watch as Liverpool took the title with Ipswich second and us third. Considering it was early days for a new manager and a new team it was not bad at all and augered well for the future. The biggest disappointment, from a team point of view, was our results in cup competitions. It was a case of those old familiar faces, with Spurs putting us out of the League Cup, winning 1–0 at home and away, while Watford, now in Division Two, confirmed their result over us the previous season by beating us again, this time in the FA Cup at Vicarage Road. It was not the only time Watford put one over us that season for they also beat us for the FA Youth Cup in the two-legged final, winning 3–2 at Old Trafford and drawing 4–4 on their own ground. I saw the first game of this smashing final and was very impressed by our two strikers, Welshman Mark Hughes and young Irishman Norman Whiteside. Both revelled in the atmosphere created by two sides committed to attack by managers Ron Atkinson and Graham Taylor, plus a crowd of almost 8000.

It was to be a while before Mark was to make it, forcing a number of extremely expensive strikers to warm their backsides on the substitutes' bench. But Norman, who bears a striking resemblance to the comedian Russ Abbot, had already made his début at the ripe old age of 16 as a substitute against Brighton. He went on to make nine full appearances in the First Division, signing as a professional in May and then going straight off to Spain to play for Northern Ireland in the World Cup Finals, becoming the youngest player to perform at this level and taking the record from Pelé himself.

It was always clear that he was going to be something special when he came over from Belfast. We had been hearing stories about this amazing goalscorer since he had been 13 and none of us was disappointed with what we saw when he arrived. I honestly thought that he would be a permanent fixture for United for the next ten years but a cartilage operation set him back a great deal. Many blame the slight dip in his form to playing so much football that first season with the emotional experience of the World Cup tagged on at the end of it. Don't be fooled, he can look after himself and that World Cup was something he would not have missed for anything. The World Cup was weighing a lot heavier on minds other than Norman Whiteside's at Old Trafford that season.

It was a season of great change with the introduction of three points for a win, instead of two, being the biggest. Although I am essentially a traditionalist, this was a step forward as it put an extra premium on winning. The full impact was not realised at the time but it is now and the benefits are being reaped by the supporters. With managers aware that a win is better than two draws, we are seeing more high-scoring games and some great entertainment. There are already people who would like to take the experiment further by introducing extra points for goals but, as far as I am concerned, that is something for the future. Let us get used to three points for a win first and see how we go from there.

Another step forward to which I have no objections is the advent of sponsors, providing they are reputable companies. For the life of me I cannot see why there was so much hesitation for many years. The officials of the Football Association, in particular, buried their heads in the sand when clubs were crying out for extra finance. I do not understand why it took so long for football and television to agree to teams wearing their sponsors' names on their shirts, after all there have been advertisements around the grounds for some time while motor racing and other sports have long relied on outside money to fund their events. Manchester United sensibly jumped onto the bandwagon with their £500,000 deal with the Japanese electronics company Sharp.

As for me I felt that the year had not been a good one. I had a bad start, was dropped and then, after my form had returned and I had signed a new contract, I suffered the knee injury against Hungary at Wembley immediately afterwards and struggled for the rest of the season. At that stage I had no idea of the mounting problems I would face during the following season, all I was concerned about was that I would miss the pinnacle of achievement for any professional footballer, playing for his country in the World Cup Finals.

10

England: From Revie to Robson

World Cups were far from my thoughts when I made my international
début. In fact the venue could not have been closer to home as Don
Revie called up Gordon Hill, regular Brian Greenhoff, and me to
play in the last Under 23 game against Hungary on Manchester United's
own Old Trafford ground. It was all something of a lost cause as the
team had lost the first leg of this European Championship game by
three clear goals in Budapest against a clearly superior side and, with
six new caps in the side, we were hardly expected to close the gap, score
four goals and reach the semi-finals of the competition, particularly after
Fekete had increased the Hungarians' lead 21 minutes into the first
half in Manchester.

It was a good opportunity for everyone to stake their claims for the
senior squad, especially with maestro Don Revie sitting up in the Old
Trafford stands among a 20,000 crowd that provided a tremendous
atmosphere. Revie, who was looking after the senior team that week,
popped his head round the dressing room door and told us to enjoy
ourselves, which we did. Jimmy Case levelled the score within a minute
of the Hungarian goal and then we set to work. With Ray Wilkins,
then with Chelsea, and Graham Paddon, an over-aged player, calling
the tune we demolished them in the second half and missed enough
chances to have won the competition outright. As it was we did not go
in front until 16 minutes from the end when Gordon Hill delighted his
fans in the ground with a superb volley. Graham Paddon made it 3–1
with six minutes to play and, even that late, we made and missed
enough goals to have pulled back the deficit.

There was no time to form an impression of Don Revie that night
for his after-match visit was as brief as his pre-match chat. He just had
time to say well done and he was on his way back to London and his
senior professionals. Every player in the country at that time had their
own idea of what this formidable man was like. His success at Leeds

in building them up from nothing had shown how single minded he could be and everyone always remarked on his complete professionalism.

He must have noticed me on that March night in 1976. I had no illusions about the reasons for my selection as there were a few missing through club calls and injuries and the inclusion of a trio of United players was certain to attract a decent gate in a tie that had basically been written off. I did not win any Under 21 caps as the switch came at the wrong time as far as my age was concerned, but I was drafted into the senior squad following our FA Cup exploits at the end of the following season and, to my great delight, I was told I would be going on the summer tour of Brazil, Argentina and Uruguay.

Even though I had watched England lose at home to both Wales and Scotland I entertained no high hopes and told myself that I was one for the future, there for the experience and that I would not be playing. It didn't matter. Here was a wonderful chance to see three South American countries I had long wanted to visit and, what was more, I had my Manchester United room-mate Brian Greenhoff to keep me company. I went on the trip determined to enjoy myself to the full. When we left Gatwick, taking off at the second attempt, we were without Don Revie and the party was being looked after by the late Les Cocker who had been The Don's assistant at Elland Road and with the national team.

So far as the players were aware, and the FA officials, Revie was away on a spying mission, watching our World Cup qualifying opponents Finland. It was even more James Bond-like than that for the England manager was, in fact, negotiating a contract in the United Arab Emirates where he moved to after causing a major storm by walking out on England in the middle of their World Cup qualifying campaign. We went out to Brazil feeling low after a spate of bad results and Les wisely didn't follow the usual strict build-up adopted by Revie and allowed the boys to relax in the Rio sunshine, swimming, sunbathing and even playing tennis and golf.

I was glad that there was no carpet putting or other party games for, as a new boy, I felt embarrassed by this sort of diversion in London and all I ever wanted was to get eliminated so that I could go back to my room to read or watch television. It may have been a little different had I been in the squad a few times before but I was a newcomer and felt it. All I was concerned about was working hard and creating a good impression, without trying to curry favour, and to improve my chances of that first England cap. I had never been much of a sunbather and my summers had been spent playing cricket rather than tennis. I had the odd swim in the pool but was quickly put off bathing in the sea when I saw my room-mate Greenhoff have the skin taken off his back when he was hurled onto the shingle by the force of the waves. I'm a strong swimmer but that frightened me. So instead I tried to maintain my level of fitness by jogging, usually with television commentator John Motson.

Not everyone felt the same way about the team. Gordon Hill seemed a lot more interested in the tennis than the football and he was not quite fitting into the squad scene. After a long chat with Les Cocker it was decided that he had a bad back and should return to England with the injured reserve goalkeeper Joe Corrigan. There was more than one sigh of relief – except from Joe who vowed that he would take two powerful sleeping tablets rather than listen to Gordon chattering all the way back on the near 20-hour flight.

No England side had ever beaten Brazil on their own soil and we were expected to be well and truly put in our place. Personally I was delighted to have even trained in the famous Maracana Stadium though I would have liked a better seat from which to watch England miss three great chances while they surprisingly dominated the first half. A long season and jet lag, not to mention opponents such as Edinho, Cerezo, Zico, Roberto, Rivelino and Paulo Cesar, saw the Brazilians take control completely in the second half when only three superb saves from Ray Clemence and two goal-line clearances from the equally outstanding Trevor Cherry kept England level in a creditable goalless draw.

Everyone had perked up by the time Revie arrived in Argentina. It is amazing what a good result can do for you, especially added to a 22-mile journey from Ezeiza International Airport to Buenos Aires city centre. The Argentine authorities were concerned about security as it was only a year away from the World Cup Finals. We were given a huge armed escort and every side road was blocked as we sped along the main road. It was a spectacular convoy and made us feel rather special. Nothing happened, of course, and the Press, in a separate bus, were entertained by their black-leathered outrider performing acrobatics on his bike. But an air of tension surrounded the place and it was not helped when the head of security presented us with one of his personal business cards and told us to show it if we were in any trouble.

Don Revie did little to alleviate the tension. He was extremely on edge before games but still insisted on helping to massage the players' legs just as he had done at Leeds. I felt he then infected the players with his nervousness. As a manager now myself I try to be as relaxed and blasé as possible even though I'm keyed up inside. I know that if I rubbed the players I would pass on my feelings. Knowing now that Revie had already decided to quit as England manager and accept the Arabs' generous offer, I find it amazing that the games still meant everything to him. He was certainly not going through the motions and meant everything he said in his emotional team talk. He was playing for real. That was the sort of professional he was as I was soon to discover to my cost.

We were not aware at the time of how seriously the home side and their supporters were taking this friendly in Buenos Aires. We thought the hostility was simply a backlash from the 1966 World Cup Finals in England when Rattin had been sent off and Sir Alf Ramsey had described them as 'animals'. The headlines called us 'Pirates' but none of us realised that this was because of the Falkland Islands and if you had taken a poll among us I doubt if anyone even knew where the Falklands were at that time. The stadium, known as the Chocolate Box, was intimidating in itself with its steep sides and its terraces so close to the pitch. By the time our team ran out the ground was covered in ticker tape which was a sight to become familiar a year later.

The players, however, reacted well to the Revie pep-talk and we took the lead through Pancho Pearson. Although Bertoni equalised from a free kick we deserved a win and you would not have placed a bet then on Argentina winning the World Cup instead of Brazil. In the end we were cheated of a possible victory when Bertoni punched Trevor Cherry in the mouth and was sent off. Unfairly, Cherry was given his marching orders as well.

Buenos Aires was a vibrant, exciting place made more attractive by some of the most beautiful women I have ever seen anywhere in the world. It became even more memorable when Don Revie came up to me at the Aeroparque before our short flight to Uruguay across the River Plate to tell me he had been so impressed by my attitude that I was not only going to be a substitute but that he was going to give me my first cap by bringing me on in the last 20 minutes. I was delighted and had to tell someone and promptly picked on poor Trevor Francis.

It was a bitterly cold day and Revie kept to the same team in a bid to set an English record of surviving a tour of South America without defeat. It was a poor game, one of those matches in which no one is ever going to score no matter how long you play. Secretly I was quite pleased as I thought it would increase my chances of getting on. I was sitting next to Trevor Francis on the substitutes' bench, listening to Don and Les shouting instructions and waiting to be told to warm up. As the second half progressed I kept looking at Trevor who would look at Don and then back at me but nothing happened. I even went so far as to start shaking myself down as I sat on the bench waiting for the signal. Twenty minutes to go . . . fifteen . . . ten . . . it finally began to dawn on me that I was not after all going to get that longed-for first cap. I have never felt so disappointed, even Trevor looked sorry for me knowing how excited I had been.

When the final whistle went I just sat there, staring into space. Revie must have seen me because he came back and said that he couldn't have brought me on in the circumstances. That was how much he wanted to avoid defeat and even knowing it was his last game he couldn't bring himself to say, 'What the heck, give the kid a chance'. It showed how professional he was and only now that I am in management do I realise what was going through his mind. He probably did not even remember his promise and, more than likely, does not now. I called him everything under the sun at the time and I even remember telling Joe Royle that I would willingly surrender every penny I had earned on the tour (around £1100) to be at home at that moment. I was disillusioned by the man. If he had just told me I was going to be substitute, I would have been quite happy because it was a step nearer. But to offer my first cap and then snatch it away was unkind.

I was very depressed during the long flight home, and sat watching Joe Royle and Emlyn Hughes playing cards for every minute of the trip. My mood was not improved when we missed the shuttle to Manchester. There was a wait of five hours for the next, so Phil Neal and I hired a car to drive us home. In all I had been travelling for 30 hours and I went to bed at midnight and slept for 15 hours.

I must say that I was amazed when I read of what Don Revie had been up to while we all thought he was away in Finland. I considered it was very sneaky and underhand and, I am sure, if he had his time again he would do it very differently. He had taken a tremendous amount of criticism over the recent defeats, particularly the one against the Scots, and he must have felt that he wanted to leave very badly. Maybe if he had talked to the Arabs following our three good results on the South American tour and after a holiday with his wife Elsie, he may have felt differently. His emotions had ruled his head and, at that crucial moment, he was particularly receptive to the offer. It was sad because it not only ruined his reputation but also damaged the Football Association's. In terms of world football it is vital that the England manager possesses the qualities of a diplomat.

When Revie turned his back on England it was left to Ron Greenwood to pick up the remaining pieces of England's bid to qualify for the Argentina World Cup Finals. He was initially appointed as caretaker for three matches, beginning with a friendly against Switzerland and followed by the remaining Group Two matches against Luxembourg and Italy. Ron turned to the highly-successful Liverpool team for seven of its players but even they could only draw with the Swiss without either side scoring.

To qualify England needed to run up a high score against Luxembourg and then beat the favourites, Italy, by a large margin at Wembley. Unfortunately England won only 2–0 in Luxembourg on a disgraceful evening when our so-called supporters wrecked the little stadium and a large part of the Grand Duchy. By then the newspapers had started to push Peter Barnes and me as the likely lads and, sure enough, we were both in the squad for the game against Italy along with Bob Latchford, who had scored 30 goals for Everton the previous season. After greeting us, Ron Greenwood quickly brought us back to earth by saying, tongue in cheek, 'I had to pick you two after all that has been said in the papers.' This time, however, I didn't build up my hopes too high until I heard him read out my name on the team list the day before the game. I was extremely nervous before the game, particularly remembering my experience with Juventus in a European club game. But I need not have worried, the Italians knew that we had to score a hat-full against them to upset their chances and they took their 2–0 defeat well.

Looking back, however, the night was one of the highlights of my entire career. I walked out of the tunnel at Wembley and felt hugely proud that I was representing my country. It may sound clichéd but pride was exactly the right word because that was the emotion I felt for my family, friends and all the people who had helped me on my way. Cups and trophies are tremendous but it is playing for England which is the thank you that these people want. It may seem corny but, before that game, my whole football life flashed before my eyes.

I was fortunate that the larger part of my international football career was played under the auspices of a man like Ron Greenwood. He was ideally suited to the task, the type of football person who should be England manager. For a start he was vastly experienced, with a thorough knowledge at both club and international level. Almost as important was the fact that he no longer needed the day-to-day involvement of club football which, for me, was Don Revie's undoing as I do not think he ever shed the Leeds way of doing things from his system.

Some national managers, for example, Revie throughout his brief England career and Bobby Robson at the start of his, are desperately keen to get full value out of every minute they have their players together, never leaving them to their own devices. In contrast Ron Greenwood was very relaxed, treating players like grown men unless they showed that they needed discipline. The odd one or two would stray but often they were players on the fringe of the team who would quietly drift out of contention. On one occasion some of the more senior players stayed out a little late at a Tottenham nightclub and the story reached the papers. Ron smoothed the story over in the Press but then, when he got the culprits training, he belittled them in front of everyone else which is one thing no player likes. It was much more effective than his giving them a dressing-down in private. He certainly did not object to the lads having a drink. Before a game we would meet at 6 p.m. on a Sunday evening at West Lodge Park in the Hertfordshire countryside, have dinner and then he would say 'Off you go to the White Hart then and pick the team for Wednesday.'

Greenwood was also tolerant and a good listener. His honesty was also much appreciated, not only by the players but also by the rest of the staff. Everyone knew exactly where they stood with Ron. If he was going to leave you out of the team he would always come up and tell you personally, often giving you the reason why. It happened to me a few times and I know that it made it a lot easier to accept. It is even more important at that high level than in club football where younger players have to learn to cope with being in and out of the team. Greenwood's failings? There wasn't anything you could point to as a major weakness. Some critics accused him of allowing his coach Don Howe too great a say in the selection of the teams, even during the World Cup in Spain. That was not true. Ron would certainly listen to advice but, in the end, it was always his team which ran out to play.

No wonder, then, that the Football Association by-passed a lot of top names and, after much publicised interviews, appointed Ron Greenwood full-time to the task of managing England for the forthcoming European Championships and the World Cup. I like to think that, maybe, I played a small part in that for, after the Italian game, everyone raved about the return of wingers and with Ron staying it looked as though Peter Barnes and I would get a chance. We did.

Barnes, then with Manchester City, came in and played magnificently. He looked great, taking on defenders, using his pace and skill and giving opponents something new to think about. It was an outstanding period, marvellous to play in and, so I am told, great to watch. England, at last, had an attacking team and I felt we were really achieving something.

Kevin Keegan was at the peak of his playing career then, a source of inspiration to everyone, and had formed an almost telepathic link with his close friend Trevor Brooking. Ray Clemence and Peter Shilton were two outstanding goalkeepers and we were also solid at the back with big Dave Watson winning everything in the air while Trevor Francis was an exciting player up front. We were confident, well balanced and best of all we were playing entertaining football.

Mind you I could have lost my part in it during the very next match when, on a snowy night, we lost 2–1 to West Germany at their Olympic Stadium. Our team gave a great performance and we were desperately unlucky to lose 2–1 to a late free kick from Rainer Bonhof. I cannot explain it but I looked around that night and felt overawed by the stadium. Needless to say I did not play at all well and I waited to be told so in next morning's papers. Fortunately no one singled me out and I can only suppose that the team performance and my one contribution, the centre from which Pancho Pearson scored our goal, carried me through.

Even though we had not qualified for the World Cup we were playing against some of the favourites and next came the mighty Brazil team, who were favourites to win the trophy in Argentina in the summer. They played rough and tough that night but we kept with them and earned a draw when Kevin Keegan scored direct from a free kick after Trevor Francis had been on the receiving end of one of many fouls. We maintained our good run with an excellent 3–1 victory over Wales at Cardiff and a scrambled single goal win over Northern Ireland. We were then ready for the big one, Scotland.

The Scots and their fans were overjoyed that they were going to South America when we were not and, to listen to their manager Ally MacLeod, they only had to turn up to win it. They were all keyed up for this game which was to be their big send-off and we wrecked it for them. I had really been looking forward to the game. I could not wait to see Hampden Park, the scene of so many great matches, the huge stadium that bulged with thousands of excited Jocks. However, I felt distinctly let down by the ground and the impression was not helped by a scrappy game. But we defended well with Dave Watson and Emlyn Hughes playing as if their lives depended on it.

I barely had a kick, so closely was I marked by Manchester City full-back Willie Donachy. Before the game I asked our coach Bill Taylor, who held the same position at Maine Road, what Willie's weaknesses were. I thought he was refusing to tell me when he said that Willie didn't have any. That day he was right. But, seven minutes from the end, I scored my first goal for England and I remember it as if it was yesterday. Trevor Francis went up with goalkeeper Alan Rough for a Peter Barnes cross and the ball fell for me on the half volley. I stretched out a leg and can remember hoping against hope that the ball would not go over the bar. After it had gone in I turned round and leapt straight into the arms of Trevor Brooking. I had not realised what beating Scotland meant to some of our players, but there was Emlyn Hughes, who had gone off injured, dancing onto the pitch while even the quiet Trevor Cherry was going berserk.

Having played poorly I thought it would go unnoticed again after scoring that goal, but when I went downstairs for breakfast next morning, my Dad passed me the papers in which MacLeod was quoted as saying that the second worst player on the pitch crossed for the worst player to score the only goal. From that moment on I felt the same about the Scots as Emlyn and I was delighted when they failed in Argentina. I'm only human, after all.

What is more I am convinced that if we had gone to South America instead of the Scots we would have done much better. They went out with three dreadful Home International Championship results behind them while we were on top form as we proved when we beat yet another of the finalists, Hungary, 4–1 at Wembley a few days later. We did not just beat them, we slaughtered them. Winning competitions like the World Cup is all about peaking at the right time and it doesn't matter how you get there as long as you give yourself the chance.

At least we had the European Championships to look forward to with some confidence. We were drawn in group one with Denmark, Eire, Northern Ireland and Bulgaria, with friendlies against Czechoslovakia, Sweden, Austria, Spain, Argentina and Australia, as well as two Home International Championships, thrown in for good measure over the two-season period. Our confidence was well founded for, on the way to the European finals in Italy, we dropped just one point against the Republic in Dublin and lost only to Austria, 4–3 in Vienna in a cracker of a friendly, and 4–1 to Wales in Wrexham when an 'experimental' side (including me) were nothing short of disastrous.

There were some marvellous matches apart from the defeat by the Austrians, including our opening 4–3 win over the improving Danes, a three-goal romp against Bulgaria in Sophia on a sweltering day and a satisfying 3–1 win over the Scots. There was also a very good European Championship win over the Irish in Belfast when we stayed overnight in the trouble-torn city as UEFA insisted. Every player was given the option of going or staying with no strings attached and, of course, no one refused. There were the usual nervous jokes but such are United's ties with Ireland that my club-mates and I were carefree, remembering the fabulous times we had been given in the past. We said thank you with a super 4–0 win.

As if to prove it was no fluke we thrashed the luckless Northern Ireland 5–1 in the return at Wembley as we suddenly began to make the rest of Europe sit up and take notice. The team was going through something of a change with Peter Barnes having lost his early sparkle and some of the senior players pushing for a more orthodox set-up with solidarity midfield. It did not affect me, however, and I was enjoying a good run in this successful team. Ron Greenwood was kind enough to come out and tell the Press that I was the first name on his team list. I wasn't, of course, as I am sure that Kevin Keegan and either one of the goalkeepers Clemence or Shilton, took the distinction. But it was nice of him to say so. The only problem was that from the moment he said it I was in and out of the side like a jack-in-the-box. It was just like the manager of a struggling club getting a vote of confidence from his Board of Directors.

Ron always had a good reason when he did leave me out saying he was trying this or that and I accepted it as long as I was included for the big games. I was more than happy to play against Spain at Barcelona in March 1980 which was undoubtedly one of the finest England performances I have taken part in. We scored after only 16 minutes when I sent Tony Woodcock away for him to show his pace and score a fine individual goal. I had one disallowed because of a push by Ray Kennedy before we clinched the game with a classic goal. Phil Thompson headed a clearance which was passed from Wilkins to Coppell, to Francis whose pace and shot provided the occasion for a memorable party that night at the famous Los Carocales restaurant off Las Ramblas.

If anyone still had any doubts that we were favourites in Italy we banished them at Wembley when we beat the World Champions Argentina, Maradona and all, 3–1. David Johnson, replacing the injured Trevor Francis, scored twice with Kevin adding the other. The result was made more impressive by the fact that Diego Maradona was at his best, with snatches of play far and above anyone else's on the field. I watched him in those opening stages and wondered why someone didn't go for him. I tried and found I couldn't get near enough to him because he was so quick. I use the past tense deliberately here because this talented young man, who should be the best footballer in the world, sold his soul to first Spain and then to Italy for cash. He does not play out of love or enthusiasm for the game any more and that is why he is far from being the best.

We quickly recovered from that awful performance against the Welsh by beating Scotland 2–0 at Hampden. Even without Kevin Keegan we won comfortably with Trevor Brooking following up his goal for West Ham in the Cup Final with another against the Scots while I scored the second – my third in successive matches – against the 'auld enemy'.

We were totally relaxed when we gathered for the finals and I was convinced that we could go all the way and win it. We were experienced, in form and confident as we headed out to our Italian headquarters in Asti and our first game against the regimental Belgians in Turin. However, it turned out to be a disaster. We suddenly found ourselves struggling to break down their defence and when we did, with an outstanding goal from Ray Wilkins, they came straight back at us to equalise through the rangy Jan Ceulemans.

The English fans' reputation had preceded them and the Italian police were ready and when the fans reacted to Belgium's goal they came in with everything, including riot shields, sticks and, worst of all, tear gas which drifted slowly across the terraces, onto the pitch and into our goalmouth where Ray Clemence was left coughing, spluttering and wiping his eyes. It would have been very easy to blame the hooligan element among the supporters for our failure but it just wasn't true. We struggled to break down the Belgians' off-side trap and simply did not repeat the form that we had been showing for two seasons.

Certainly the crowd were well enough behaved when we returned to Turin three days later to face the host country in front of 60,000 of their own fans. We lost 1–0 to a Tardelli volley and I was held partly responsible for the goal, having dived in to tackle the skilful Antognioni as he set up the move which carried Graziani past Phil Neal to cross for Tardelli. All I had planned to do was stand up to the midfield player and shuffle him inside but I was right in front of our bench and I was aware of Ron Greenwood shouting at me telling me to tackle him. I should have followed my own instincts.

We moved on to Salerno for our last group game against Spain in Naples and, after two bad performances, I was not included as Ron made a few changes, using 19 of his 22 players. We won 2–1 but it meant nothing and when Belgium drew with Italy, we were not even in the play-offs for third and fourth place. I have racked my brains asking myself what went wrong with the team and me but have never been able to come up with a plausible solution. All I can suggest is that had we played Italy first it might have been a different matter because Belgium were a spoiling side and knocked us out of our rhythm before we had begun. Ah well, there was always the World Cup to look forward to!

We thought that at least qualifying for Spain would present no problems. Famous last words. We were drawn in Group Four of the European section along with Romania, Hungary, Switzerland and Norway. With two teams going through under the new system there seemed to be no danger as we started off by thrashing Norway at Wembley with four goals. Not even a defeat by Romania in Bucharest, when I came on as a substitute for the nerve-racked Eric Gates, warned us of the disasters and miseries that were to follow. It was a close thing as we squeezed past the Swiss at Wembley and were then held to a draw at home by the well-disciplined Romanians. We knew that we now needed a good return from our short summer trip to Switzerland and Hungary. The omens were not good when we set out for Basle, as we hadn't won in our last five matches and the papers were screaming for the heads of the managers and the players.

We missed three chances at goal and a penalty before the Swiss went into the lead against the run of play through Scheiwiler. It was the old one, two, for within a minute, Egli put Sulser through and we were two down. Although substitute Terry McDermott pulled a goal back, our first in eight hours of international football, we lost and, effectively, England had, once again, failed to qualify for the World Cup Finals. The media were quick to criticise us for not only had we lost on the field but, also, our supporters had disgraced themselves again. We did not even know of the troubles as players arrive at the ground an hour before the kick-off, concentrate on what happens on the pitch and by the time they leave the fans have all gone.

We trained hard for the match in Budapest after Zurich – and how we worked. Criticism from the Press is a great motivator while the desire for survival was the driving force, not for our manager Ron Greenwood, who had already made up his mind to retire, but for ourselves and our own futures. Phil Thompson and Phil Neal joined us after winning the European Cup with Liverpool against Real Madrid in Paris and that probably helped Ron decide to go for experienced players.

Before the game at the famous Nep Stadium there was a match featuring yesterday's stars and I stood next to a huge and sweating Ferenc Puskas in the tunnel before their kick-off. He looked anything but a legend until he stepped onto the pitch. Even at his age and weight he was in a different class, scoring a hat-trick without hardly moving; I don't know if he was supposed to be an inspiration to the Hungarians, but we were the inspired team that day. We got off to a lucky start when I just managed to toe-end a pass through a Hungarian's legs to Terry McDermott who in turn set Trevor Brooking up for a shot he mis-hit into the net.

The Hungarians turned it into a test of stamina when Garaba scored just before the interval and, if anyone had seen our dressing room at half time, they would have given us no chance at all as Mick Mills and Trevor Brooking underwent emergency treatment from our doctor, Vernon Edwards, and physiotherapist Fred Street. It was touch and go whether or not they would restart but they did and not only that but Brooking, who was not the highest of goalscorers, scored a second goal of such power that the ball lodged behind the stanchion. Kevin Keegan clinched it for us with a third when he was brought down in the area and took the penalty kick himself.

We were jubilant but the mood quickly changed on the flight back to Luton when Ron Greenwood quietly announced to the players that now we were on the threshold of the World Cup Finals, he planned to retire and allow a younger man to take charge. We were astounded and the senior players quickly put their heads together and went to Ron to try and make him change his mind. Happily he did, but he cut it finely by doing it just minutes before the Football Association were due to announce it to the unsuspecting Press in the baggage claim area at Luton Airport.

I suspect he wished he hadn't when the new season opened. All the good work we had done in Hungary was lost in Norway where, though we had a goal start, we lost. I was absent through an ankle injury and watched the débâcle on television with almost tears of frustration. Once again it looked as though we were out, but Switzerland came to our rescue by taking three points off Romania and as we came to our last game against the Hungarians, we knew exactly what we had to achieve. Even the public forgave us, the media firmly supported us and Paul Mariner's goal gave us the trip to Spain. I was euphoric, despite the pain of my injured knee though I would not have been had I a crystal ball. The injury, of course, left me uncertain about my place in the finals themselves but I was determined to make them and received full support from Ron Greenwood. I played the full match against Scotland and then had my final fitness test against Finland. I was happy enough when Trevor Francis took my place during the game and the manager quietly asked 'You OK?' I nodded and was on my way to Spain.

Playing in a World Cup finals was very important for me and I was immensely relieved that I had made it. What is more we went as a side used to playing with each other and had started to put our football together at just the right time. The preparations were perfect and a credit to Ron Greenwood and his staff. There was some criticism over the choice of our hotel in the industrial northern port of Bilbao particularly when photographs of the beach in front of it, amid the depths of winter and covered with a variety of rubbish including a dead dog, appeared in the papers. By the time we arrived it looked in very good condition having had a spring clean. After all this was not the Costa del Sol and if a foreigner complained about the holiday hotels and the beaches in Bootle or Birkenhead they would be laughed out of court.

Our hotel, Los Tamarises, was quite satisfactory and the owner, called Jesus, could not have done more for us. The food was excellent and the recreation facilities more than adequate. A delightful personal touch came when Jesus presented us each with a bottle of Rioja from the cellar he called his 'wine museum' which corresponded to our dates of birth. Ron's bottle must have been a bit special!

We also had the use of Bilbao's excellent training camp and when we came to face France in the opening match we were in marvellous shape, even though we were without those room-mates Kevin Keegan and Trevor Brooking, out with a back injury and a sore groin respectively. If anyone was worried it didn't show for we made World Cup history with the quickest goal on record as I took a throw on the right, Terry Butcher back headed it and Bryan Robson scored after 27 seconds. Although the talented French came back to level we went on to win 3–1 with a second goal from Bryan Robson and a third from Paul Mariner. We gave an awful lot in that match and because of the heat, our heads were spinning at half time, necessitating large quantities of cold blankets and salt tablets to be brought in. It showed in our next game against the Czechs, which we won 2–0, and we hardly looked any better in the one-goal victory over well-drilled (forgive the pun) Kuwait.

A lot was going on behind the scenes as the West Ham doctor was flown in to give Trevor Brooking an injection in his troublesome groin; Kevin Keegan crept off to Hamburg without being missed by the Press to see his osteopath while Joe Corrigan was sent home with a suspected torn cartilage in his knee, only to return at a later date. The remarkable point about these problems was the fact that, even though some of us had close friends among the Press, no one breathed a word, everyone was completely loyal to the manager which was indicative of the respect and esteem in which we held him.

Ron was preoccupied with the injuries and other difficulties and this was why he was quick to accept a request from the Royal Ballet company to meet the players. He was delighted to have an added distraction and arranged that they should present themselves on Press Day. It could easily have turned out to be another disaster for one look at the girls, all of whom were rather top heavy, disproved the 'ballet' claim and they turned out to be go-go dancers from a local disco.

It gave us all a giggle and we moved onto Madrid for the quarter-finals where we were to play the West Germans and our hosts Spain. Everyone kept telling us that the West Germans were not on form and ready to be taken, and it was said that we would never have a better chance. But even a poor German side are always going to be physically strong and they held us to a goalless draw in the Bernabeu Stadium in a poor match. We ran out of steam when we needed that extra push. The Germans then beat Spain 2–1 and we knew that we had to win our game against the Spaniards by two clear goals to qualify for the final.

But, by then, the World Cup for me had already ended. I finished the game against the West Germans experiencing no more pain than normal and the next day I went to play a round at the local golf course to relax and unwind. I played the first three holes and then my knee started hurting. I stopped playing and decided to walk it off but the more I walked the worse the pain became and it began to swell up immediately. It had got no better two days before the Spanish game and I was nowhere near fit and it was decided that I should be given a steroid injection. It worked wonders and I was even able to train a few hours later.

A second injection next day was almost a formality after the success of the first and I was a willing patient. That night there was a game on television and we all crowded into the lounge to watch it, as this is the best kind of break to the monotony other than actually playing in a match yourself. Suddenly I began to feel sick and was sweating so badly that I quietly slipped off to my room in the middle of the game to lie down. By the time my room-mate Phil Neal came up I was in a dreadful state as I had suffered a reaction to the second injection and Dr Edwards was promptly called to give me a shot to send me to sleep.

I wished I hadn't woken up for when I did, the team had been announced and I was out. I jogged later and it didn't feel too bad but this was for a place in the World Cup Final and not even Keegan and Brooking, who had both declared themselves fit and ready to play, could get beyond the substitutes' bench. It was the only decision Ron could have made.

The rest is history. Neither side could score even though both Kevin and Trevor were to make their long-awaited appearances with 27 minutes to go and both missed great chances. It was argued by many, including the two players concerned, that since they were fit enough to be substitutes they were fit enough to play but it is always easy to say that with hindsight and it must be remembered that Brooking did not play again until the following March. It was a tricky decision and had it worked Ron Greenwood would have been hailed a genius and probably have earned himself a knighthood. Obviously Kevin was disappointed because he was always a winner and no one cared more about England than he did. Who would have guessed that it would be his last full appearance for England.

Personally I believe that Ron Greenwood did all he could with both Kevin and Trevor. He was right to let Kevin go to Germany as that was the only way Kevin thought he could get himself fit and he was right not to rush him back, for it was not impossible that we could score two goals against Spain without him.

What sticks in my mind, however, is how close the top teams were. Brazil were undoubtedly the best team, but were beaten by Italy, while the second-best team was probably France whom we beat 3–1. Had they or, indeed we, reached the final anything could have happened. It is only then that you realise how close we came. We finished undefeated, but out of the competition and I do not think any other manager could have done a better job.

Like Joe Mercer who was briefly in charge, Greenwood was the right age and had the right experience. Obviously you need to train more seriously at international level but at senior international level you don't need to train constantly. There needs to be discipline but a little freedom and to be treated as an individual is important as well. I was only in two squads with Bobby Robson because of my injury problems but the change in atmosphere and attitude was immediate and startling. Having been used to more freedom under Greenwood the training suddenly became very intensive once more even down to sessions on Sunday and staying in somewhat spartan conditions at our new training centre, Bisham Abbey.

Robson was, of course, settling in at the time and learning the subtle difference between managing at club and international level. He was treating those three-day gatherings like a club manager and was anxious to use every second. There was not a revolt but there were some murmurings among the senior players who had been used to different ways and people found excuses not to train, particularly on the Sunday session. A lot of professionals, me included, value that 24 hours after a game to recover and relax. At that stage of our careers we know our own bodies best and how to pace ourselves.

The new manager, however, showed a couple of great qualities in those early days for he not only listened to players' problems but showed he was flexible and prepared to make changes. I am sure that the move from the luxury of West Lodge Park to Bisham was forced on him by the powers-that-be at Lancaster Gate to save money but when he found how much we disliked it we moved five miles up the road to the comfortable High Wycombe Crest and continued to use the excellent facilities at the Abbey.

Another of Robson's early errors of judgement was to axe Kevin Keegan from the squad in the way he did. I appreciate that Kevin had not played a lot of football because of his back injury that had curtailed his playing in the World Cup and also that Bobby wanted to stamp his personality and authority on his first squad. But I am sure that if he had the chance again he would do it differently. Even if Bobby did not plan to use Kevin he could have called him up because we all liked to have Kevin around. Even if he had told him that he had no part in the playing future of the team he could have used him in some capacity and I am sure Kevin would have appreciated the chance.

We were used to him being there, not just on the field but off it as well, going to him for advice on so many things such as commercial deals, while he would always have a word for those who needed it as we prepared for games. A letter or a telephone call might have done the trick but, at the same time, Kevin should have been big enough to bite his tongue and await developments. Kevin was impulsive and should have given a new manager, picking three squads at that time, his chance to come back and explain but Kevin shut the door in his face by saying he would never play for England again.

It would be unfair for me to judge Robson's capabilities after the two starkly contrasting games I played in (a 9–0 win over Luxembourg and a soulless, goalless draw with Greece at Wembley). His first few sessions, understandably, were too man-managed. He has, quite clearly, learned and is now much more relaxed.

I feel no bitterness or resentment that my football career was ended because of a bad tackle in an international match. After all, it could have happened at any time in any game. My only regret is that I did not manage to win 50 caps. That, to me, would have been very fulfilling although I should be satisfied with 42 when I look at some of the good players, like Jimmy Greenhoff, who never won a single cap.

When I signed that first contract to play for Tranmere I thought no further ahead than football paying for my next couple of years at university. I still maintain that I was never an outstanding player but that I worked hard and recognised my limitations as well as what I was capable of doing. All in all I am delighted at what football and England gave me and if a wish could be fulfilled it would be to have those 50 caps and a League Championship medal.

There has been a great deal of discussion over enthusiasm, or the lack of it, among England players. I never found that to be the case and I do not think that those who play for the Scottish, the Irish or the Welsh have a scrap more enthusiasm than we do, it is probably just that they are more emotional while we tend to be a little more reserved. I will say, though, that you need at least ten games to feel part of the international scene. It has nothing to do with any cliquishness or coldness on the part of the players, it just takes time to feel you belong.

Even Kevin Keegan reckoned that it took him a dozen games and look what a great player he was for his country. Passion, power, talent, he had the lot and was respected by every player. I was fortunate to have played with him and some very good international footballers while I was with England and none more so than Liverpool full-back Phil Neal. He was often the target of some vitriolic sniping from the detractors who embarrassed me by saying that I helped him out. Phil didn't need my help and was one of the best passers of the ball in the game. I felt extremely comfortable playing with him and every time I dropped back to help out he would reciprocate by coming to my aid when I went forward.

I also had great admiration for Trevor Brooking, somewhat of an anomaly, and quite the opposite of what you would expect a footballer to be. He was more like a country squire and, indeed, we called him *Hadleigh* after the suave television character. He possessed terrific skills and wonderful vision, not to mention one of the most infectious laughs in the business. Then there was the appetite and enthusiasm of Emlyn Hughes and the quieter dedication of my regular room-mate Dave Watson who must have gone round the world four times as reserve to Roy McFarland before taking his opportunity superbly. He fully deserved to win so many caps and receive rightful recognition.

Bryan Robson and Ray Wilkins are excellent midfield players whose styles complement each other; both would run through brick walls, if necessary, for their country. The debate continues as to who is the better captain. Ray is the better talker, he is even bossier on the pitch than Kevin Keegan, but Bryan, like Kevin, leads by example. There is no question at all about his stature as a world class player.

Then what about the two keepers, Peter Shilton and Ray Clemence. Shilton is the hardest worker I have ever come across and is totally committed to being the number one goalkeeper in the world. Clem, in many aspects, was his opposite, relying on his natural ability but, in his own way, also determined to be recognised as the best. If I was forced to take my pick I would have to choose Shilton but there is really nothing between them. If I was asked why I picked one against the other I could no more tell you than some of the managers who have been faced with the same happy problem.

At one stage I came in for criticism from the United fans who claimed that I played better for my country than I did for my club and I have to admit that there was an 18-month spell when it was true. Mick Mills and Phil Thompson were two other England players who suffered the same criticism. They both had those great qualities of stamina and consistency.

Glenn Hoddle is a different sort of player altogether but I feel sure that when he recovers fully from the injuries which occurred just as he was set for a run on the international stage, he will become an integral part of the team. With no shortage of good players, it begs the question why have England done so badly since winning the World Cup in 1966? For my money it is because the English League will not make sacrifices to the English national team. In many respects the priorities are right. We have the best League in the world for that very reason. But even with our crowded fixture list there could be a much better marriage between the Football League and the Football Association.

Bobby Robson had the right idea when he took the opportunity to try and organise a talk-in during a relatively empty period between World Cup qualifying matches only to be foiled by the weather. I am certain that the Football League could ease off a little to allow the England manager a clear Saturday before those more obviously important World and European qualifying matches.

Club managers could also be more helpful. It is not unknown for a manager to pay a player not to take the risk of playing for his country. The oldest instinct in the world is that of survival and now that I have had some experience of managing a club I can see why they do it. Not allowing a player to join his international team when the player has an injury is understandable though I must say that Ron Atkinson did not bring any pressure to bear on me after my knee injury. Bobby Robson in fact, twice sent me back to the club for treatment and I hope that this attitude of give and take is picked up by the club managers. What I don't like is the hypocrisy of certain managers who pay lip service to Bobby Robson and the England team, do little to help and then go on television and earn money for voicing their criticisms.

There must be a day of reckoning when the League and the Football Association decide on their priorities. The England manager, at the moment, is not getting a fair crack of the whip. Even without this assistance we rank within the top six in the world and if the manager were helped a little more I could see England taking that vital step forward into the top four and challenging once more for the trophies, or at least the medal stages.

If we can bridge that gap then the League will feel the benefits, as they did in 1966 when gates improved after England's success just as they did in Italy after their World Cup triumph. Success at the highest level is a shot in the arm the game would love to have but it is not success by Scotland, Wales or the Irish but only by England.

I certainly believe that Bobby Robson has the necessary qualities but he can only be as good as his players. Fortunately there are people like John Barnes, Bryan Robson and Ray Wilkins. There is the goalkeeping of Peter Shilton, the defensive abilities of Terry Butcher and Kenny Sansom, and the peripheral players like Mark Hateley and Glenn Hoddle. It provides the framework around which the manager can fashion his side – injuries and club managers permitting.

11

Final Season

Opportunities to play for England in my last season were limited to just two matches as we touched the heights with a nine-goal massacre of Luxembourg and then plunged to the depths in a desperate goalless draw with Greece at Wembley, a result which eventually cost us our place in the finals of the European Championships in France that summer. However, I wouldn't have been involved for my season, and indeed my career, came to a shuddering halt at the end of the game against Sunderland at Roker Park early in April. The only consolation was that I went out at the top, the dream of many sportsmen, playing international football and helping my club to two Wembley finals in one season. It was, in fact, a momentous season in every way for me.

After an indifferent beginning I played some of the best football of my career, certainly on a par with the 1977–78 campaign which I always had thought of as my best. I was not even certain of starting the season for it was only a matter of five weeks after the most recent operation when I laced on my boots and tried out the suspect knee in a reserve game against Arsenal. I scored and felt good enough to tell Ron Atkinson that I was ready to give it a go.

We opened the season against Birmingham City at Old Trafford in front of 48,673 spectators, winning by three clear goals with me scoring one of them. I played in those first half dozen games but two games a week was simply proving too much for my knee and it soon began to deteriorate. I went back to see the specialist in Cambridge and he told me to cut down my training. That was easier said than done. I had never been a naturally gifted player, but rather the sort who needed to train and one of the talents I was given was a capacity for hard work.

It was decided that the leg muscle was not good or strong enough to take the workload that was being required of it and so it was agreed all round that I should take a couple of weeks off to build up my quads and my strength. When I returned I gently eased back into the action during a demanding spell of our programme, playing against sides like Liverpool and local rivals Manchester City. I was aware that I was not 100 per cent fit and made a conscious decision to take greater care and to avoid the sort of challenges I had been used to.

I managed to fall into a routine and towards November I felt that I was playing quite well. I was using my soccer intellect instead of my legs and making the most of my experience to save unnecessary running and strain. To my surprise and delight I discovered that my brain was quite capable of looking after me. Other and better sportsmen than me have found that an injury is a wonderful way to channel the mind. Golfers have won the Open Championship with bad backs and cricketers have scored centuries in Test matches with broken fingers because they have had neither the time nor the mental capacity to consider factors such as the opposition or the conditions. You concentrate on your injury and playing to the best of your ability without causing further damage.

I couldn't have done too badly for, after missing three games, the manager kept me in the side and I was also firmly included in England manager Bobby Robson's plans. Robson, in fact, was extremely helpful and very understanding. On a couple of occasions he realised that I had little chance of being ready and sent me back to Manchester to work on my fitness, and like Ron Atkinson, never forcing or demanding that I should play when I did not feel well.

Apart from my knee – and the ominous news from Cambridge that I would need another operation at the end of the season – there was plenty to occupy my mind with Manchester United making the headlines daily for one reason or another as the team climbed to the top of the First Division, announced a loss of £2,282,007 and were knocked out of Europe with an UEFA fine for crowd misbehaviour to go with it.

I have mentioned before that, more often than not, footballers know little of what their fans are up to until they read about it in the newspapers but the day we lost 2–1 to Valencia in Spain we witnessed first-hand the events which led up to the club being fined more than £1000. How often have you heard supporters returning from an incident abroad claiming provocation? It is easy to nod your head knowingly and believe the worst but, in Valencia, it was the absolute truth. We drove up to the stadium to be welcomed, as usual, by our supporters who stood around the stationary coach chanting and singing waiting for us to disembark. It was the normal scene that is seen at every ground we appear at and yet the Spanish police, for no obvious reason, drove their horses in among the English men and women supporters, forcing them away from the coach. This was bad enough but worse was to follow as flying hoofs were followed by swinging truncheons. At that moment it was easy to understand how a normally unaggressive person could snap and fight back. I am sure I would have done the same under those circumstances.

There was a drastic need for the lines of communication to be improved, especially abroad. I have witnessed before the anti-English feeling in Spain, especially when England played in Madrid during the World Cup, when there was bad feeling stemming from the Falklands conflict. Whatever the reason, there was trouble after the game and as I read about it and watched the television reports when we got home I wondered, in this instance, just how much our fans were to blame.

The fine was no more than a drop in the ocean but even that was unfair, penalising the club for the behaviour of their supporters, over whom they had no control. Not even the announced £2 million loss caused any great tremors along the corridors of power at Old Trafford. As far as Manchester United were concerned it was an investment in players which was bound to be repaid.

While other clubs look to their directors to find the necessary cash to fund their plunges into the transfer market, it is the fans at Old Trafford who buy the Manchester United players. They turn up in their thousands week after week and even in the Second Division they averaged a gate of over 40,000. How many other clubs could count on such loyalty when they have not won a First Division title for more than 15 years?

There were some bad moments during the season, not just for me and that worsening joint, but also for my team-mates. My close friend Ray Wilkins shattered his jaw against Bournemouth in the Milk Cup while Ashley Grimes was sent off and found himself at the centre of a Football Association inquiry for bringing the game into disrepute. Poor Ashley is hardly a villain and no one's idea of a hatchet man but, at

West Ham, he was sent off for pushing the referee. It was all done in the heat-of-the-moment and the best way to describe Ashley's action is as a slight prod as he tried to make his point. He was wrong and, quite rightly, was sent off. Where he was unfortunate was that the Football Association were in the middle of a clean-up campaign and he was one of 120 sent off by the end of November. An example had to made of someone and Ashley was the fall guy. In the end, because of the publicity, he was fortunate that he was fined only £750 and suspended for two games.

As the Chairman of the Professional Footballers' Association I was involved in discussions with the referees at that time and I supported their attempts to try and cut down on the cynical and professional foul. It was a pity that UEFA, the European ruling body, did not follow the lead that our Football Association took. Everyone complains that the standard of refereeing has fallen and yet no one is prepared to do anything about it. For absolute control referees need the respect of the players and that comes from authority. Strip them of that and there is no discipline.

Ray Wilkins' injury had nothing to do with referees or foul play. It was just one of those unfortunate accidents that can happen, but this one had remarkable repercussions. I was only five yards away when Ray collided with Phil Brignull and the noise was so sickening that I had to turn away. It resulted in a nasty operation with all sorts of wires needed to pull the cheekbone back into shape. At the time of the accident Ray was captain of both Manchester United and England – and a very good one, too. Ray was replaced in both jobs by Bryan Robson and Ray was not to resume his captaincy. At the time I thought that it was wrong because I considered Ray was the better captain and that the extra pressure on Bryan would affect his game. Now, with the benefit of hindsight, United manager Ron Atkinson was absolutely right because Robson handled the added responsibility superbly, becoming a more authoritative and commanding player.

Ray, however, is a natural leader, able to help and encourage others without it affecting his game at all. When he first arrived at Old Trafford he took a lot of stick from the crowd. A groin injury did not help and neither did some of the comments from his own manager Ron Atkinson about his square passing and branding him 'The Crab'. But, typically, there was not a murmur from Ray. On every occasion he knuckled down and got on with his job. But Ray was the midfield general, the linkman who gave 'Pop' Robson the freedom to go forward.

I believe that, in the end, everyone appreciated just how good Ray was but, for some, it took the £1.7 million transfer to AC Milan in Italy to convince them. His move almost certainly enabled United to resist the temptation to sell Bryan Robson to Italy, helped Ron Atkinson rebuild the side and paid a substantial amount towards the redevelopment of the offices at Old Trafford. What United lost was not just a commanding player but one who may have helped them fill those empty spaces in the trophy cabinet. It is my belief that if Ray had stayed and played with some of the new signings, United would have cleaned up the following season. Because of his injuries and his inability to win back his place in the side Ray played only 26 League games that season which probably explains why our Championship challenge to the inevitable Liverpool failed. They went into the lead by mid-October, stayed there and had tied up the title long before the end of the season. It was infuriating as we would beat the top teams and lose to those at the bottom. It was inconsistency personified and the same problem United faced the whole time I was with them.

Out of Europe, out of the Championships challenge, all that was left were those Cups again and we set about winning them with a vengeance. The Milk Cup, as the League Cup had become that season, came first. We had fancied our chances in the past only to come unstuck for no apparent reason. This time we had a good run through to the semi-finals with only the odd hiccup such as Ray's injury at Bournemouth, in a tie we had already won in the first leg, and a testing goalless draw at Bradford City whom we eventually saw off 4–1 in the replay before beating Southampton 2–0.

We really began to fancy our chances when we crushed highly-rated Nottingham Forest by four clear goals at Old Trafford. It is a strange thing but, in recent years, Wimbledon manager Dave Bassett has been saying how he enjoys winning against Brian Clough, having done so on several instances, including Milk and FA Cup ties. Now, I do not know Clough personally but such is his public image and amount of exposure that I also felt an extra kick out of beating his side. It is, I am sure, a case of his own publicity rebounding on him as he motivates opposing teams and managers as much as he does his own players.

The win earned us a semi-final place against Arsenal with Liverpool drawn to play Burnley in the other. We went to Highbury on a frosty night with Arsenal as the tipsters' choice to beat us. We were devastating, and gave the most dynamic performance any United team has yet produced for Ron Atkinson. We had the benefit of an early goal from Norman Whiteside on the glassy surface and then proceeded to demolish the Gunners in front of their own bemused fans. That first strike came after about 12 minutes which is the best timing possible at an opponents' ground. Any earlier and it is considered a bit of a fluke but, by the time we had scored, we had assessed the pitch and our opponents and we were able to relax. In contrast Arsenal's game was a bit frantic. Within an hour we were four goals ahead after I had found the net twice and Frank Stapleton had added the other against his old team. All would have been idyllic but for the fact that we let down our guard and allowed Arsenal to come back into the two legged semi-final with late goals from Tony Woodcock and Peter Nicholas.

Ron Atkinson could not believe his ears when he came into the dressing room to congratulate us on our fine victory. The smile froze on his face as he walked into what must have seemed like a major row as we criticised ourselves for giving away those two late goals. As it happened it didn't matter for when Arsenal came to Old Trafford they knew that they were a beaten side. They desperately needed an early goal but it was United that scored first as I netted my sixth goal of the competition. Although Raphael Meade scored for Arsenal, Kevin Moran got another for us and we were back at Wembley on a 6–3 aggregate having been watched by almost 100,000 fans in our two semi-finals.

We did not come out of a physical game unscathed, however, as our captain Bryan Robson went off with a badly injured ankle which was to keep him out of the final and, indeed, out of football until 9 April. This was another reason why our League form lacked consistency. Ironically it was Ray Wilkins who came on as the substitute for the injured Robson against Arsenal to resume the captaincy of the side. It was cruel that Robson should have to miss the final against Liverpool at Wembley. It would have been his first and we all felt for him as Wembley is every professional footballer's ultimate goal. Although he had played there many times for England no one could ever say for sure that a player would be back for a Cup final. The team, of course, missed his driving, forceful qualities in the final itself when we lost 2–1 to Liverpool after extra time.

The game confirmed my belief that the team that win a cup have their name on it from the start. Even without Robson we fancied ourselves when we stopped Liverpool in their tracks with a twelfth-minute goal from Norman Whiteside. Was this going to be a repeat of our semi-final victory over Arsenal in London? Not a chance! Everything ran against us and just when it looked as though we might last out the game, full-back Alan Kennedy scored one of those vitally important goals he seems to reserve for big occasions. A lot of critics blamed our goalkeeper Gary Bailey for that one but I have to admit to a share of the responsibility. I ran out to close Alan down and thought I had any possible shot covered. He hit the ball which flew past me, past Bailey and into the net. I could not believe it when I looked back and saw the ball in the goal. I had miscalculated my positioning by about a yard and gave Alan that vital sight of goal.

Ronnie Whelan scored a magnificent winner in extra time but, by then, our game was a shambles with Kevin Moran having hobbled off and our other centre back Gordon McQueen limping out on the wing with a pulled hamstring. Our emergency centre backs were Frank Stapleton and Mike Duxbury with Lou Macari in the unaccustomed role of right back. Although it was no disgrace losing to a side of Liverpool's ability it was still a shattering experience, more so for the rest of the team than for me as I had something else to occupy my mind. I was to make my maiden speech as Chairman of the Professional Footballers' Association at their annual dinner and awards at the Hilton Hotel in London.

As it turned out no one needed to worry for Manchester United had tasted cup fever and were soon provided with another route to Wembley, via the FA Cup. It is amazing how often, these days, clubs enjoy good runs in both competitions during the same season. The reason is that players get a feel for knock-out games and become confident. If I were looking for a team to tip in the FA Cup these days I would look at the Milk Cup results first as a pointer.

Certainly that season we all felt we would win the FA Cup with our own performances and others' results strengthening that belief. We beat West Ham, Luton and Derby County without conceding a goal but it was after we beat Everton in the sixth round while Liverpool were losing to Brighton that we were convinced. Everton played really well at Old Trafford with goalkeeper Jim Arnold stopping everything we could throw at him and they looked set for a deserved Goodison Park replay where they would be favourites.

There was probably no more than a minute remaining in our game when we won a corner and manager Ron Atkinson, with a last throw of the dice, pulled off the nearest man, Mike Duxbury, and sent on substitute Lou Macari. He ran straight into the box, and headed the corner down for the limping Frank Stapleton to volley a superb goal. It was one of those flashes of inspiration that are hailed as match winners. Most of the time they don't come off – but then most of the time your substitute is not called Lou Macari!

By one of those coincidences which occur so often in football the semi-final draw of the FA Cup paired us, as for the Milk Cup, with Arsenal. The difference this time was that it was a one-off affair to be played at Villa Park and also that Steve Coppell would not be playing. But, at that stage, I was still involved and shared in the atmosphere and build-up having played in every round and scored a couple of goals. Any misgivings I had disappeared as I watched the lads recover from Tony Woodcock's first-half goal to win with efforts from Bryan Robson and Norman Whiteside. But, by the time Wembley came around, the situation had changed. I was a mere spectator and knew it, no matter how hard the manager and the rest of the team tried to bring me in. In fact, I made a big mistake by travelling with the team to their Cup Final headquarters at the Compleat Angler in Marlow. I would have been better off staying away.

After my retirement there were lots of stories which suggested that Manchester United were slow in reaching a settlement with me. These were all completely without foundation as Martin Edwards and his Board of Directors treated me extremely fairly when they could have got away with far less. The agreement was never straightforward inasmuch as I was retiring two years after the injury which necessitated it and that, in turn, was not helped by the fact that the injury had happened while I was playing for England and not Manchester United.

There were other complications resulting in long negotiations with the Football Association and the insurers.

I had the final operation on 30 September and United continued to pay me my salary until early December. I then stepped back and let my mate Gordon Taylor of the PFA carry on the discussions with Martin Edwards. Naturally I suffered fits of depression as I struggled to walk down my own staircase because of the pain and was also agonising over my future.

In the end all was resolved with a fair settlement as well as the promise of a testimonial game for me while United used their insurance money to replace me. They bought Aberdeen's talented young Scottish international Gordon Strachan. I have followed his career at United with more than passing interest and I guess that I shall always feel some empathy with whoever runs down the right wing at Old Trafford. I was pleased and flattered that Ron Atkinson had bought such a good player to replace me.

There was a lot happening as I tried to rebuild my professional life. The proposed testimonial provided a good distraction with Ron Greenwood typically offering to bring an England team to Old Trafford the weekend after my retirement. It sounded good but it was all a little impracticable and, in the end, the whole thing was cancelled. Much the same can be said about the job offers which I received. An insurance company, a sports goods firm, wine importers, all nice but not really appropriate. Wigan offered me the post of Chief Executive but without any real job description and I turned it down because I had by then almost decided that my next three months would be spent in Holland.

The last thing I wanted was to be a cripple for the rest of my life but, after the last operation, my left leg was so weak that I knew I would have to work hard just to be able to do the simple things in life. If I was not careful I would not only have to kiss football goodbye but also cricket, golf and many other things you take for granted when you are fit and healthy. I had spoken to our Dutch International Arnold Muhren about it and he had recommended a physiotherapist in Amsterdam called Richard Smith, a man also used by a number of top Dutch sportsmen. Richard Smith offered me the sort of deal that I could not refuse. He was convinced that he could not only help me but could also get me playing again and went so far as to say that I could stay with him for three months and if, after that time, I was still unable to play I need not pay him anything. On the other hand, if he were able to live up to his promise I would pay him ten per cent of my earnings from the game in future.

I was realistic enough not to get too excited by his promise but the prospect of just getting fit enough to live a normal life and the thought of three months away from familiar surroundings to think about the rest of my life won the day and I packed my bags, slipping out of the country like a fugitive with only a handful of people knowing what I was up to. The story, if anyone discovered my whereabouts, was that I was studying Dutch football and their coaching methods. If that had been true I would not have needed three months. I did go and watch games but all it did was show me how lucky we are in England. Their League is so boring with just three or four good teams and the rest part-timers. The standard was poor and the football not at all entertaining. The only similarity was the crowd violence which I witnessed at first hand when Richard Smith had his nose broken at a local derby after complaining that someone was in the seat for which he had a season ticket.

During the whole time I was in Amsterdam there wasn't a moment when I believed that I would play professionally again but I was doing the sort of exercise which I would never have had the will power to do on my own at home. Richard Smith was a difficult man to work with. He worked extremely hard and demanded from all those around him the same sort of dedication and commitment he had had in building up two successful clinics at the age of 28. His methods of treatment were unconventional. He used the Cyrriax method and would fiercely rub the affected area. The therapy was deep and extremely painful in the early days.

Looking back, the improvement was immense but, at the time, I did not fully appreciate it. I was beginning to feel homesick and my situation was not helped when Smith spoke at length to an English journalist despite having agreed that there would be no publicity until after the treatment. There was still a week remaining of the three months but as I was returning home for the PFA Dinner, I told him that I would not come back. It meant we parted somewhat unhappily which was a shame for he had shown me tremendous hospitality, opening his home to me, accepting no money and really doing a fine job on my leg. But, no matter how much longer I stayed with him, I was never going to play top grade football again and one more week was not going to make any difference.

The time had come to accept that I had to return to England and find a job to keep home, body and soul together. There had been lots of nice pieces in the newspapers saying how well qualified I was to take a top job with either the Football League or the Football Association. It was also rumoured that Manchester United were about to offer me employment. But those sort of jobs do not suddenly become available overnight and there was never any contact with either the FL or the FA though I was offered a job at United. It came not from Martin Edwards or Ron Atkinson but from the restaurant manager Jim Barker. I had often talked to him and told him that I was quite interested in the catering trade. He told me that he planned to retire in a couple of years' time and if I fancied learning the ropes I could take over from him. It was a genuine offer which I really appreciated but somehow I could not envisage myself waiting on customers in the club restaurant on match days. It just didn't seem right.

In any case I had decided that I wanted to stay in football and I gave myself until July to try and find a job to keep me in the game. I spoke to Wigan again but it was still the same situation as before, really squeezing me in and creating a job for me. There were rumours of other jobs but they were just rumours. Nothing happened.

I was giving myself every chance. Having been out of the country for three months, I attended as many of the usual end of season functions as I could to show that I was alive and available. It was at one of these functions, the Football Writers' Awards Dinner, that I first met Crystal Palace Chairman Ron Noades. To be perfectly honest I didn't have a clue who he was when he came up to me while I was chatting to the Charlton Chairman John Fryer, but I certainly knew him by reputation. After the formal introductions he told me that he had planned to offer me the assistant manager's job at Selhurst Park shortly before manager Alan Mullery was dismissed. That, of course, went by the board when Dave Bassett was appointed. Four days later Bassett sensationally decided that he did not want the job and returned to Plough Lane and his Wimbledon job. The moment I heard the news I knew that I was going to be offered the Palace job and, sure enough,

Ron Noades telephoned to invite me to London to have a chat.

No sooner did the news become public that I was to discuss the Crystal Palace job than I was urged from all quarters to turn it down. Everyone wanted to tell me what a dodgy job it was and not to touch it with a barge pole. Take something else, they said in unison, but no one said exactly what else. It was all I had. There was nothing else. My self-imposed July deadline was approaching at that stage and it was Palace or quit football. There was only one decision I knew I could make.

12

Coppell at the Palace

Crystal Palace Chairman Ron Noades is a very conscientious man. By the time he picked up the telephone to talk to me about the prospect of managing the London club he had already checked me out with Sir Matt Busby, former England manager Ron Greenwood, and PFA Secretary Gordon Taylor to mention just a few, to ask them whether they thought I was capable of doing the job. I must have been given good references, for he invited me to make the journey down to Selhurst Park to talk over his offer.

It will come as no surprise to Ron Noades that I also checked him out very thoroughly, particularly after all the warnings I had received telling me not, under any circumstances, to become involved with Palace. Football is a small, gossipy world and I had already heard stories about him and the club long before there was any suggestion that I should join them, and it must be said that not much of what I heard was good. Through the PFA, I had dealt with claims from their ex-players concerning non-payment and clearly I had to go into the interview with my eyes open. So I also spoke to as many people as I could to get a feel of the man and the place, including the manager Ron Noades had just sacked, Alan Mullery. Not surprisingly Alan Mullery told me to think very carefully before accepting the job. He told me that, because of Palace's lack of funds and huge overdraft, he had felt as if he was banging his head against a brick wall. He also told me that Ron Noades was a very difficult, demanding Chairman to work with.

I arrived at Selhurst Park armed with more questions for the Chairman than he had for me. I wanted the job but if I had found out that things had not been above board and right I would have refused it. The Chairman did not try to cover anything up and was quite open about the financial and playing difficulties at the club. It was widely said that since his arrival at Palace there had been nothing but trouble. Palace was the 'Team of the Eighties' as they had been called under

Terry Venables, and the most popular word at the ground was 'potential'. But when Noades arrived the club was in absolute turmoil and it was his responsibility totally. He accepted that.

Noades showed me over the ground and I had no doubt at all in my mind that this was a First Division ground and a First Division set-up. My instinct told me that Noades was being honest with me and laying all his cards on the table. He did not pretend that great things awaited the club around the corner and I had only to look at the League tables for the previous four years to see that I would be inheriting a team that knew nothing other than battling against relegation while my common sense told me that they were in a financial mess and were without the cash flow of Manchester United and their average 45,000 crowds.

As for his reputation of interfering – his office is in the ground – I was not worried for I knew I had an awful lot to learn and needed anyone and everyone with any experience. Hard working? He is. Demanding? Without any question but in the short time I have known him he has never asked his staff to do anything he would not do himself. He is not a nine-to-five man and he expects others to be the same if there is the work that needs to be done.

Noades puts in an awful lot more than he takes out and he has the good of the club at heart in every decision he takes. I am convinced that if Crystal Palace could find themselves a benevolent millionaire to bail them out of their current financial plight they would enjoy success with Ron Noades as Chairman – under me or whoever was manager at the time.

Despite my obvious inexperience Noades never questioned my decisions or tried to interfere with team selection, indeed he often did not know the line-up until the team ran out onto the pitch. He always, however, asked the reasoning behind decisions, and that is how it should be. I never found him deliberately obstructive, only helpful though it was always a developing relationship, with the responsibilities only loosely defined.

He is one of the new breed of Chairmen who wants to be involved in the day-to-day running of the club. Why not? He has an obvious and deep regard for the game having qualified as a referee and having also attained his preliminary coaching badge with the Football Association. He is football crazy, as I discovered just before I assumed my duties at Selhurst Park. It had been a beautiful summer's day and when I telephoned him at his home that evening I asked him if he had been sunbathing with his family. No, he replied, he had been watching a kids' five-a-side competition to see if there was a youngster worth following up. He takes his share of the scouting duties and is no fool when it comes to judging a player's ability. But the facts have to be faced that he has hired and fired seven managers in the space of seven years. Something has to be wrong somewhere. And caution was the keyword in that first season of management.

For someone who likes to foster an image that makes people wary and often frightened of him, Ron Noades is remarkably open with the media. He is always available and always ready to talk. This has caused me some personal heartaches particularly when we sold Peter Nicholas to Luton Town for £165,000. I must be honest, I did not want to sell him but circumstances necessitated it and, for the first time in six months, I found myself with money to spend on players. The only problem was that our Chairman was immediately quoted in the *Daily Mirror* as saying just that and immediately every player I approached suddenly had a few thousand more added to his transfer fee. Ron Noades had been talking to a football writer in what he thought was an off-the-record chat. He was let down and it rebounded on me. The bad weather of that season swallowed up all the cash to pay the salaries. But then Ron Noades would also talk to any supporter who knocked on the window at the ground, often spending up to half an hour explaining the ins and outs of the club to a man who had come to criticise him and his team.

Personally I was grateful for the work that the Chairman was prepared to put into the club for there are some staff shortages when you owe £150,000 a season in interest alone to your bank. When I arrived the scouting staff consisted of my assistant Ian Evans, the Chairman, John Griffen – a taxi driver who used to do the early shift so that he could go and watch a game for us in the evening – and me. The reserve and youth team manager was even more of a surprise. His name was Alan Smith, a comfortably-off director of a London property development company. He looked as though he would be more at home in our boardroom than on a muddy touchline. But I could see straightaway how enthusiastic he was. I have no doubt at all that if

Smith devoted all his time and energy to his chosen career he would be a very rich man but he loves football so much that he is at his Covent Garden office at 6 a.m. where he spends three hours working hard before driving to our Mitcham training ground where he takes the lads for a session before going back to his office in Central London. Added to that he takes the youngsters two nights a week. Smith is a workaholic and, more importantly, he cares about each and every player in his charge.

The task of management did not daunt me. I said all along that all I wanted was a chance and this was it. I was prepared to ignore my misgivings and the question marks. I was not frightened of failing and, inwardly, I hoped that my arrival would act as a catalyst to the future growth of the club. I'm sure every new manager feels that. When the Chairman and I agreed the terms of the job he asked me if I had anyone in mind for an assistant. To be honest I didn't as I had originally hoped that my introduction into the other side of the game would be somewhat more gradual and that I would be the number two to an experienced manager who was going to show me the ropes. I mentioned that I admired Michael Docherty's integrity and felt that I could work with him. It was then that Ron Noades suggested former Palace player Ian Evans, a Welsh international whose career, like mine, had been cut short by injury. I could see the advantage of having someone who knew Palace well and as soon as I met 'Taffy' I knew we would get on. We had similar ideas on the game but were interested in different areas and so would complement each other well.

I was under no illusions when I began the job and, indeed, when I took over I told the Board that a team which had struggled at the wrong end of the table for so long would not be transformed into promotion challengers overnight. I was right, the better players had begun to drift off with Billy Gilbert having already joined Portsmouth while, to my regret, Vince Hilaire was determined to move and went to join David Pleat at Luton.

Football management is an all embracing discipline. Everyone who goes into the business has their own ideas to put into practice, which are variations on a general theme which you think will make the difference between you and the other 91. Reality soon brings you down to earth. Nothing is simple and it is a question of picking it up as you go along. I had no grand master plan to bring the European Cup to Selhurst Park in five years. I had ideals based around Manchester United and Liverpool and I knew you could go some way towards them with time and patience but those are two commodities which are not readily available.

The first thing to strike me at Palace was that everyone was living in the past. The ill-chosen word 'potential' still dominated everyone's thinking along with the players and crowds of more than four years ago. Terry Venables and Malcolm Allison were still being talked about. The reality was a £1.3 million deficit which, without that benevolent millionaire, could only be reduced to sensible proportions by shrewd financial and football management. I was told that there was a limited income from our excellent promotions department and that I had a chance of a small share to spend but with interest demands coming in thick and fast it was soon diverted.

There was only one thing for it in face of the myriad of problems and that was a cautious approach. If I had gone in heavy handed, generally throwing my weight around, there would have been civil war in the dressing room – and that was the last thing we wanted when we were beginning a season trying to stop the rot and avoid relegation. I have to confess that I was extremely nervous inasmuch as I suddenly found myself at the helm of a very large business with absolutely no experience at all. A lot of people were relying on me to pay their wages and I was concerned that I did not want to let anyone down, least of all myself.

I certainly did not need a degree in economics to tell me that Palace's overdraft and the bank's refusal to raise the limit meant I would have to develop a youth policy to replace Alan Mullery's emphasis on experience. The club had not been taking in youngsters of 13 and 14 and so there were no young players ready to challenge the seniors for their places. I stood back and took stock of the situation and I was not particularly pleased. Some players on the staff commanded no respect at all and were happy picking up inflated wages while playing for the reserves with no ambition to move on or to try and make first-team football. Quite clearly we were not going to become a good side overnight with players who had struggled at the bottom of the Second Division since being relegated from the First. I was able to replace the two outgoing players with striker Trevor Aylott from Luton and former Everton winger Alan Irvine but before I could add to that I had to reduce my staff and to do that we had to make settlements with certain players.

Having been involved with the PFA it was strange to find myself suddenly on the other side and I came to the conclusion that there was a lack of tolerance on both sides. The players could not and would not see the problems the club faced while the Chairman showed no sympathy when salary payments to players were paid late. A little give and take can go an awful long way and a happy club and dressing room can obviously strongly influence what happens on the pitch.

One thing which did impress me was the help I received from managers in the game. It is like a club within a club. The managers are friendly, stick together and are always ready to give advice. As a player you don't know it exists but when first going into management it is almost heartwarming to find this camaraderie in such a competitive and cut-throat business.

A classic example was Manchester City manager Billy McNeill. The only time I had come across him before was when I sat on a tribunal to discuss City's attempt to sack their winger Peter Bodak for a breach of discipline. I was the PFA's representative on the three-man tribunal and though because of industrial law it did not reach the stage of personal opinions being expressed, I felt sure that he would hold me responsible for the punishment having been reduced to a two-week suspension. I did not see Billy again until we met as opposing managers in my first season, when I thought he would bear a grudge against me. He was extremely helpful, sympathetic and charming. What is more he has not been the exception and those managers I have had cause to approach have given me honest and genuine opinions. I talked often in that first season to my old bosses Dave Sexton and Ron Atkinson while I knew that others such as my former international managers Ron Greenwood and Bobby Robson were always available if I wanted to talk to them. I telephoned big John McGrath one day about one of his players at Chester and we spent almost an hour chatting about the game.

I admit I needed that help early on, as I took those first few steps in management. I spent one afternoon talking to a goalkeeper I wanted as cover for George Wood, and the whole time I kept thinking that there was something wrong. I could not put my finger on it but it hardly mattered as he priced himself too high for my budget. It was a good job he did for I suddenly realised what was bothering me – I was trying to sign a boss-eyed goalkeeper. What a start that would have been!

Another player who interested me in those early days was the Brighton defender Eric Young who, I was told, had come to the end of his contract and was in dispute with his club. I telephoned my old mate Joe Corrigan to find out what was happening and he confirmed my opinion that Eric was a good player who could give us a great deal of help. Fortunately, Joe said, Eric had given him his phone numbers a couple of days earlier and he was happy to pass them on to me. I tried the Brighton number first and, getting no reply, I dialled the London number. It was Scotland Yard and I quickly replaced the receiver than ask if I could speak to Eric Young. To this day I don't know whether it was Eric winding Joe up or Joe winding me up.

I was learning the hard way and when I did succeed in buying my centre half from a notable First Division club I had to send him back when he got into trouble with the police! Another to get away from me was Cardiff City midfield player Gary Bennett. I wanted that boy badly but, at £65,000, Sunderland were quick to step in and give him the chance of First Division football and, within a matter of months, he was valued at £250,000.

Beggars cannot be choosers and our limited scouting staff scoured Britain in search of the right players at the right price. I personally watched games from the Isthmian League Division Two up to the First Division and travelled from Plymouth to Kilmarnock and Dublin to Southend. I watched games in all four divisions, the Southern League and the Alliance, and I would plan my week by looking at the fixture list. In my first six months as a manager I watched almost 100 games. I used to think of Crystal Palace as a London club but one of my major drawbacks of the job was the distance I had to travel as it took me an hour just to get onto the M1 Motorway and with my woeful lack of knowledge of the roads around London I seemed to spend more hours in my car than anywhere else.

It was even tougher on my wife Jane. Having been in Holland for three months I was only back home in Cheshire for two months before

I was off to live in a flat in London while she looked after our house, her job and her sick father. If we had a weekend match in the north I would stop off in Cheshire, otherwise she would catch the train to London on Friday night. On a typical weekend the uncomplaining Jane would arrive at Euston on Friday night, we would grab a quick drink and snack in a wine bar, getting back to Surrey in time for me to make my telephone calls and for Jane to do the laundry. On Saturday I would be off to football while Jane would go to the shops to buy my weekly groceries, clean the flat and look for a house. Providing the game was not too far away I would be back in time for her to cook dinner. On Sunday morning I would call in at Selhurst Park to see if there were any injuries from the day before and then, if I was not due to watch a player in Ireland or on a local park, we would look at more houses before I drove her to Euston in time to catch the 6 o'clock back north.

Added to all that I am a bad loser and more often than not returned home in a foul mood after suffering the latest set-back. Those were the black moments when I would wonder what the hell I was doing in the job. In that position you have to have self doubts and I did not know whether I was tackling the job in the right or wrong way, whether my decisions were good or bad because I had nothing to measure them by. As time went on I felt that I was capable and able but it was a matter of whether I could learn quickly enough.

The job itself was exactly what I had envisaged and there were no surprises. When I joined I had yet to really break away from United and I suppose a little part of me will always be Old Trafford. For the first couple of games I was an outsider looking in but, very quickly, the job overtook me. I saw how much the club meant to so many people – supporters who spend so much of their time and money following the team, others who work voluntarily for the club and those within the club itself. I soon put United away and my sole concern became Crystal Palace with the events at the club dictating my life and my movements. Football is a demanding game and you have to be passionately involved or not at all.

Players have little idea of what a manager's job involves beyond what they see him doing at the stadium or training ground. I know that when a manager isn't at the club everyone automatically assumes he has had enough and has decided to take a couple of days away from it all. Not just me and not just Manchester United but players at all clubs talk about Brian Clough or Jack Charlton making an appearance at the club only once or twice a week. I can now understand why those training sessions early in the week are often left up to the assistant manager or the coach. It is because the manager, more likely than not, has driven half a day to get to the other end of the country to watch a player, and has then driven back through the night to clear up some office work.

I was fortunate that Ian Evans is completely wrapped up in the fitness and coaching side of the game. There is nothing he likes better than becoming engrossed in a training session with the lads while I prefer the managerial side, probably because of my economics background. I also feel that I can learn more by standing back and watching, albeit from a short distance. One thing I can understand now is how football can and does get into your blood. I felt it first when I came back from Holland and knew that I had to try and stay in football in one capacity or another or I would regret it for the rest of my life. Now football has become such a part of me that it is hard to shake free. I have some qualifications which could help me find a job outside the game if necessary but football will always hold an attraction unless I am convinced I have nothing left to offer it.

13

Blueprint for Success

I consider myself extremely fortunate in having been able to experience so many aspects of this great game of ours in such a relatively short time. I have played at both club and international level, as a part-timer and amateur with Third Division Tranmere Rovers, then with Manchester United in their promotion year from Division Two and finally in the World Cup Finals in Spain with England. I have seen the heartaches and problems of fellow players during my year as Chairman of the Professional Footballers' Association and now have seen life on the other side of the fence as manager of Crystal Palace.

My privileged positions have given me sufficient insight into the game to reach the conclusion that would-be reformers should keep their hands off football and leave well alone. There is nothing wrong with the size or structure of the game in England and talk of forming a Super League leaves me cold because we are in peril of the big clubs doing just that without help from anyone else. I see a Super League as the greatest danger facing the game at present with the large clubs getting larger at the expense of competition – the very thing on which the Football League is built – and for this reason I am completely opposed to home clubs keeping all their gate money. Ninety-two clubs may not be ideal but the structure of the League has survived for 100 years without major change and not many other sports could boast that as well as having become an integral part of local communities. Whatever the changes that have occurred in society, football has always seemed capable of mending its ways and adjusting.

Norman Chester's second report on the Future of Football recommended a Super League but, if current trends continue, it will have already evolved of its own accord and would comprise the clubs that have the incomes to headhunt the best young players from the smaller clubs. If clubs follow the Liverpool example of signing Wayne Harrison from Oldham for £250,000 after a handful of first-team games and then lending him back to Oldham, there will be no need for the top clubs to spend their money on youth policies. Have we seen the advent of nursery clubs kept alive by big brother? The Harrison arrangement may have worked well for Oldham but it does not follow that all the smaller clubs will be as successful in turning up their own prodigy. What will happen to the little clubs that fail to produce the potential young superstar in an otherwise successful youth scheme which suits their own needs?

As a manager I soon discovered how hard it is becoming to entice the bright young men of the game to a club which isn't in the top bracket. In the past you could promise these kids a much earlier break-through into first-team football and the possibility of a financial killing with a big transfer if they proved good enough. These big clubs have now hardened their attitude against this and offer the young players a three-year contract with the promise to pay the players off in full if they don't make it.

The only way to combat this is to increase the minimal four per cent levy of gate money that is kept by the home club to a more realistic figure such as ten or twelve per cent. It would not particularly hurt the top clubs but it would certainly help those that are struggling. Some critics point out that the small, badly-supported clubs should be allowed to disappear and leave a stronger League but it is remarkable the way small football clubs have managed to keep going. There is a great will to survive and even when the taxman or a major creditor forces a club to the verge of bankruptcy there always seems to be someone from the world of commerce ready to save them. The PFA even had the very welcome experience of Robert Maxwell of Oxford United and Ken Bates of Chelsea coming to Southend's rescue with a big loan to bail them out of their immediate difficulties.

Even more surprising, given the growing pessimism of the critics, is the fact that for every club facing bankruptcy there is one waiting to take its place. As a manager I often have cause to look beyond the four divisions and to visit non-League clubs. Many of the Alliance League clubs not only have excellent facilities but have learned to balance their books and live within a sensible budget. Clubs like Telford United, Altrincham and Maidstone could follow Wimbledon's recent bold example of leaving the Southern League without fear, if necessary.

It has been suggested that the clubs in the lower divisions should become part-time but I disagree. I believe that we should struggle on the way we are. It is a familiar argument with the 42-game season which, given the uncertainty of British weather, can cause a congested timetable and put a great deal of pressure on any club going for more than one trophy. But isn't that all part of the British game? It brings out the typical British 'bulldog' attitude by playing in mud, snow, wind and, at the start and end of each season, on good firm pitches. If you win the Football League Championship you really know that you are a team for all seasons. The introduction of plastic pitches could alter some of that but there is little danger while the type of carpet Queen's Park Rangers experimented with remains so inferior to a natural surface. I have no doubt at all that, eventually, a really good artificial surface will be developed which has all the best characteristics of grass and there will always be a club like Rangers prepared to try it out and good luck to them.

Personally I believe that football has overcome the crisis that was threatening the very heart of the game. There will always be some sort of sickness ailing such a big sport but in terms of transfer fees, gates and its role in the local community we are beginning to see the light. Having fallen dramatically, attendances seem to have stabilised so that clubs can plan accordingly and just about exist during an ordinary season and flourish in a successful one – if they have their sums right. I think that gates will improve substantially only if England wins the World Cup, a possibility rather than a likelihood at the moment, or if we are granted permission to stage either a European Championship or the World Cup itself. We certainly have the stadiums, an efficient transport system, the expertise and the crowd potential to compete successfully with any nation with the added advantage that we are usually able to deal with outbreaks of violence at our own clubs and certainly those at the larger stadiums.

The banks' refusal to provide further credit on a wide scale and the arrival of paid financial directors have together ensured that the once spiralling transfer market has been contained if not fully curtailed. But I am still not sure that we have it absolutely right. I am strongly in favour of a multiplying system for assessing transfer fees which is an extension of the method used by the Transfer Tribunal and the European Union. No method will be absolutely ideal because there must always be anomalies when trying to place a value on a person rather than a piece of machinery. A player is paid what his skills are worth within obvious limits and this figure can then be used as the basis for the transfer fee. Other factors such as age, experience, number of games in the Football League, international appearances and any other relevant information can then be taken into account. There are all kinds of permutations and with the increasing use of computers they could all be fed into one with a figure popping out at the other end.

Transfer fees at present still tend to reflect trends in the game rather than realistic sums for players but this is now slowly changing with salaried and qualified financial or managing directors using their professional judgement instead of a local wealthy butcher or whatever supporting what he instinctively thinks is right after seeing only his club's home games. Decisions such as the outlay of a large capital sum for a footballer are now based on commercial viability and what the club can afford rather than on a hunch. The same sort of financial criteria is being applied to professional football just as it would to any other business by people who have a full-time commitment to the game.

Football not only came to its senses over silly money but also in recognising the cancerous growth of hooliganism in the game. The ruling bodies have come in for a great deal of criticism from all sides because of the violent minority on the terraces but I think their response has been mature and praiseworthy though they have had little choice or it would have been downhill all the way! Like it or not clubs are identified around the rest of the country with the behaviour of their supporters, and every ground's atmosphere is created by its fans. I especially applaud the work Graham Taylor and his staff at Watford have done as Vicarage Road is a happy place, a nice ground to watch a football match where fathers can take their children and wives without feeling unduly threatened. Other clubs, like Southampton, are making a huge attempt to create a family atmosphere and that must be preferable to the feeling of suspicion and aggression that the thugs can generate. It is up to each club to look after its own.

The standing of the club in its local community is critical in controlling hooliganism with goodwill from both sides going a long way. Clubs are recognising, albeit slowly, the need for more involvement locally such as the idea, poached from Europe, of annexing basketball clubs with the same name. But that is only scratching the surface and there is a wide range of services which can be offered to local residents, whether they are bars and restaurants, supermarkets or a large variety of sports facilities. It can also be a double-edged sword for, other than making the local population more aware of a football club's activities, it could also provide a source of added income and there are very few clubs in Britain that can survive on their gates alone.

Commercial managers have become increasingly important to the modern game with their lotteries and other money-making schemes providing a crutch to ailing sides but, even so, clubs still greatly rely on the income from pools and television. I cannot help but feel, however, that the Football League's negotiating committee did not act in the best interests of their members when they signed an agreement with the pools companies for the next 12 years. However, it is done and there is no use crying over it. The answer may lie in a scheme that is being supported by many of the clubs and, if they get their way, it will see the entire 92 members of the Football League running their own pools competition. It makes a great deal of sense and would not, or should not, affect the income from the pools companies who would simply have to accept another competitor. To succeed, it would need a united effort and if this was forthcoming the platform would be built for a lucrative enterprise. All the profits could be ploughed back into the game if the competition was organised by the clubs. Even the printing of the tickets could be undertaken by someone in the game such as Robert Maxwell. The distribution system already exists with each club acting as a depot. The idea is a good one but it does need the backing of everyone and not just a handful of clubs.

Football should be careful not to underestimate the value of the income from television. The game and the two major television companies should not abuse or try to take advantage of each other's weaknesses but rather be supportive as they are reliant on each other. Obviously each party holds an opinion as to what televised football is worth and there is clearly a point at which television will slam the door and abandon football because it is too expensive. It is up to the negotiating committee to get as close to that limit as they can without overreaching it. It would be very unwise for football to call television's bluff, for if that were to happen I have no doubt whom the losers would be.

It would be suicidal in terms of advertisers and sponsors for what companies would spend the sort of sums that are currently spent on shirt sponsoring without the possibility of having their names on television once in a while and the same principles apply to the hoardings. It would leave the door open for the major crowd pullers such as Liverpool, Manchester United and Spurs to reach their own agreements. If there wasn't any football shown on television, gates would probably increase but by nowhere near the numbers needed to compensate for the huge loss of income and it would signal the end for some of the smaller clubs, especially those without the glamour to lure those essential businessmen.

The amount of soccer that should be televised is a different matter altogether and neither the television producers nor the clubs can predict the right matches to be shown on the right days. I do feel that we have enough live football and indeed I would like to see games regionalised with, say, Liverpool v. Manchester United televised in London and not screened in the north west and vice versa for Arsenal v. Tottenham. This, I am sure, would help boost attendances which, in turn, would create a better atmosphere for the broadcasters and the players.

I also sense the relationship between the game and the media in general becoming more fragile by the season. I went into management with an open mind ready to help the Press whenever I could. My reward was to be let down in the first couple of interviews and I quickly learned that there are some media people who need to be handled with great care. It seems that every paper these days has a nice man who has the good of the game genuinely at heart, a hitman, and a sports newsman. You know you are in trouble when the last-named comes to call.

The ones I cannot stand are those who make their names on the back of cheap controversy and, in some ways, I admire how the contentious Chelsea Chairman, Ken Bates, has had the courage of his convictions in banning those journalists he thinks are misrepresenting his club. However, in those circumstances you have to be very sure that you are in the right. To be fair, it is not just the newspapers that are irresponsible. Radio and television are deliberately misleading when they highlight one fight on the terraces involving a dozen people out of 50,000 who are enjoying the game and causing no disturbance. On one occasion I heard a radio commentator express great surprise that there had been no crowd trouble at a game involving a team with notoriously bad supporters. His entire summary of the match was about this one aspect and the scoreline was added almost as an afterthought. It was rather like reporting that a dog did not bite a man.

It has to be faced that there is a clash of interests between the media and those in the game and also that there will always be managers, directors, and players who feed the gutter Press with all the dirt they need. But as with television, we need each other, for after all football is the national game and just as we need the publicity, so does football help sell the newspapers.

The other controversial aspect of our game lies in the way it is officiated, and while it has to be said that the standard of refereeing could always be improved, British referees compare more than favourably with their counterparts in the rest of the world. Let's face it, although everyone makes mistakes a referee has his errors examined under a microscope. Considering the circumstances, they make the best of the worst job in sport. Players could help make it easier for them and could also prepare them better for their duties. For a start I would like to see an experiment whereby half-a-dozen officials were put onto a realistic salary to work and train together as professional, full-time referees. There would be facilities to enable them to watch videos of games and they would be given full access to watch matches around the country, so that they could bring greater consistency to their decisions. They could visit clubs, mix socially with the players and talk to managers about particular problems. The whole matter could be reviewed after a couple of years to see how much improvement, if any, had been made. If the experiment were successful then the number of professional referees could be increased.

Even if that scheme were not adopted I am glad to see officials now encouraged to form closer relationships with the players and managers. Previously they were actively discouraged from mixing and from all conversation. As a result there was much public washing of dirty linen that can be avoided now that the referee and the manager can sit and have a

drink and exchange opinions after the game. I have no doubt there will
be some harsh words but, at least it will be kept 'in house' and they might
possibly understand each other's problems.

It is often suggested that more ex-professional footballers should go
into refereeing. Perhaps it would help if the job were made a full-time
occupation but, somehow, I don't think it would. Everything is already
done to encourage professional footballers to take up the whistle. All
apprentices are taught the laws of the game, urged to continue with
their academic studies and asked to take charge of local games. But
there are not many who are genuinely interested especially when they
realise how hard they would have to work after they have finished
playing simply to make the panel for the Football League. I think
players see the referees' difficulties from too close at hand and I
personally have never had any inclination to become a referee.

Referees have a vital role to play in the future of the game and their
importance should be recognised. Similarly footballers should be more
closely involved in shaping the future of football for after all it is their
game, their living and their future. They should certainly have a
representative, such as the Professional Footballers' Association secretary Gordon Taylor, who would sit on the relevant committees to
state their case. I would also like to see the players involved in the
Football Association coaching scheme to bring them in line with most
other sports which are run, at least in part, by former participants.
However, few ex-professionals are currently involved in football's
administration.

Having switched from playing to management, I can see the need to
get together the best brains from all sides to make our game work.
One of my great regrets at having to stop playing prematurely was that
it also meant that I had to retire as Chairman of the Professional
Footballers' Association which was an office I enjoyed immensely but
one that can be held by a playing footballer only. I was first asked to
join the committee by former secretary Cliff Lloyd but I declined
because, at the time, Stewart Houston was the Manchester United
union representative and I felt that it would have been a slight on him
had I gone in above his head.

I had no hesitation in accepting when Stewart Houston left Old
Trafford and, before I knew it, I was asked to be Chairman. I jumped

the queue as I was only fourth in line at the time but of the other three contenders: John Hollins was reconsidering his playing future and talking of going into coaching or management; Bob Latchford said he would not have felt comfortable as Chairman; while Paul Hart enjoyed his involvement but could not see himself in the role either. So I accepted the position which already had strong United ties. I replaced a former player, Alan Gowling, while Noel Cantwell, Malcolm Musgrove, and Frank O'Farrell all had had links with United some time during their careers and all had been PFA Chairmen.

I was not going into the job as a reformer like two of my predecessors Jimmy Hill and Derek Dougan. My responsibility was in administration and to ensure that the members knew what was happening to their £12 a year. I knew that many thought it was money out of the window, a subscription for an annual booze-up and dinner in London. Nothing could have been further from the truth.

The PFA provides advice on just about everything related to football or for players trying to establish a career after football. Subjects outside the game itself include: further education; introductions to prospective employers after retirement; contracts; sick pay; pensions; and mortgages. Members have only to pick up the telephone or write to the PFA. Apart from the committee comprising three players, there are eight full-time staff, headed by Gordon Taylor, consisting of his assistant, three girls, an education officer, his assistant and their secretary.

As well as this the PFA retains the services of legal and financial advisers. The PFA would pay a member's legal expenses if it was a football-related matter and would give a contribution towards their costs if it was some other matter that the PFA considered deserved help. Our education people can organise anything from a cookery course to an HGV licence and often the player could claim back some of the fees. Yet despite this, during my term, players' agents would often telephone the office for help and information and then charge their clients for advice that we had provided free. It used to make Gordon furious but he was hardly in a position to start a campaign against agents and all he could do was try and 'educate' our members. The work of the PFA often goes unnoticed and unpublicised particularly when they make grants to former players who have hit on times of hardship. The Association has paid many gas and electricity bills on behalf of a once famous name who did not know where else to turn for assistance.

Normally Gordon Taylor goes quietly about his tasks but he suddenly found himself under a spotlight when he set out to help rescue clubs in financial difficulties. Some think that maybe the PFA went beyond their scope but when a club closes down it is the players who have the most to lose. It may mean that a director loses his hobby but to the 20 or 30 players it means losing their livelihood and that is why our own 'Flying Doctor' Gordon Taylor moved in to help clubs like Bristol City, Hull, Wolves, Charlton and Southend.

Fortunately the players' trade union is quite a wealthy one, though not from members' subscriptions but rather from its slice of the television fees. Even this share has come under attack in recent years but I don't see how anyone can deny the players that right when they are the stars of the show. Some people at Lytham St Annes and Lancaster Gate seem to have forgotten that without the players there would be nothing for them to administer. The agreement is with both the Football Association and the Football League and the percentage was set some years ago. The share is now a massive amount because of inflation but the PFA do not demand every penny and are content with a steady income. This is possible because no one draws a large salary and the Association is run on a shoestring with no large expense accounts. No one is trying to make money out of players.

Gordon Taylor is the driving force of the set-up and deserves all he earns. He spends his life on the telephone and driving up and down the country. He is more in touch than any other official in the game as he deals with legal and educational matters, negotiates on behalf of those players overawed by the talk of contracts and sits regularly on arbitration committees. He has continued Cliff Lloyd's good work. It is ironic when you consider that he was appointed by a management committee which, because it consists of players, can change constantly but Gordon is the stabilising influence and provides the continuity. Because of its leadership the union is a sensible body and the players have been made aware that they have more to lose than anyone else and that though they have power, it must be used sparingly.

The Spanish professional footballers have shown how they can call the tune by their recent strikes and if our players wanted to behave tyranically and take over the game they could. Fortunately, a sound relationship exists at present between the administrators and the men who play the game and a strike remains what it should always be, a last resort. There was never any talk of industrial action while I was in the chair and the closest we came to any serious action was when the Football Association and the Football League tried to cut back our television fees and called us greedy. It could have turned nasty but we had right on our side and sensible discussions ensured that a gentlemen's agreement was reached.

I would like to see Gordon Taylor take his northern common sense into many more situations. I am not saying that players should have a say in the internal politics of the Football Association or the Football League, but only that they should have a voice in anything that concerns their welfare and future. Let's face it, the days when soccer players wore a cloth cap, cycled to games on a bike and dined on fish and chips and half a bitter have long gone. There is enough money in the game to attract intelligent young men who in the past would have gone straight into industry or commerce because of the vast differences in pay and the standard of living. There are a lot of responsible players in the game with a great deal more to offer than being 'over the moon' when they win and 'sick as a parrot' when they lose.

At the same time footballers must be aware of their responsibilities both on and off the pitch. The future depends on the paying spectators and football and its players must be ready to encourage those people in any way they can. If the income is assured then we have a reasonably healthy sport.

Clubs have already started to look to improvements such as family enclosures, while the police forces throughout the country have dealt with the problems of hooliganism. The trend is now definitely towards the American style of spectator sports which attract the whole family instead of just one member of the household. The footballers must help as well. When I was at Manchester United we met the supporters halfway to encourage them to come and watch us. We visited the supporters' clubs, schools, coaching schemes and anything else where we could reach potential supporters or introduce ourselves to the local community. Image is critical not only on the pitch but off it as well. Professional footballers should be aware the youngsters copy their heroes and if the ones they look up to set a good example, those youngsters will also behave well.

On the pitch I would like to see an improvement in the petulant attitude of some of the players. No one enjoys seeing a player arguing unnecessarily with the referee. Competitive, fierce, aggressive football is fine but arguing the toss over whose throw it is or whether or not a free kick should be given is irritating and does nothing for the image of the game. Spontaneous gestures in a highly-charged First Division match are a different matter and difficult to stamp out as the ruling bodies have discovered in recent years. However, if referees were given the same powers as their counterparts in Rugby League I am sure that we would see an immediate improvement in overall behaviour. If every player who had a go at an official was penalised with a free kick, he would soon become a hindrance to his team-mates and an annoyance to the club and their fans.

Managers have been helped by the introduction of three points for a victory which is a change I salute. Managers are paid to win, not to entertain but the difference between a draw and a victory has encouraged even the meanest man to send his team out looking for maximum points.

Clubs can do much more. It is time we moved on from the days when spectators had a paddle every time they went for a pee at half-time and were served a soggy paper cup full of tea or Bovril as refreshment, while standing in the open getting cold or soaking wet, when they paid to watch their favourite team play football. If supporters are to be encouraged to pay the increasing admission charges and if football is to keep up with its competitors in the multi-million pound leisure industry, it must be ready to make its supporters feel wanted, offering them good car parking facilities, a comfortable seat and easily accessible refreshments.

There are signs that this is happening at certain clubs. The experiment at Watford's Vicarage Road has been particularly successful because they actually managed to increase their gates even though results were down on the previous season. Because of their success we will see more and more clubs reserving sections of their stands and grounds for family groups as others have played the usual waiting game to see how the trials have fared. The only drawback I can see to this laudable scheme is that by sectioning off an area of stands or terraces for normal humans, the hooligans will feel that the remainder of the ground is reserved for them.

The problem of hooliganism has been with us for a very long time but it took two particular matches to bring it to a head, when Chelsea played Sunderland in the semi-finals of the Milk Cup and Millwall travelled to Luton in the FA Cup. The violence provoked such a public outcry that the Government felt obliged to intervene with the Prime Minister Margaret Thatcher taking a personal interest, and demanding meetings with the football authorities while being instrumental in having the traditional England-Scotland fixture switched from Wembley to Hampden Park.

Personally I felt that the Government's action was unnecessary and cosmetic. They felt that they had to take steps to prevent further violence but, in the end, it will be no different from any of the solutions football clubs themselves have come up with over the years. Switching a game from London to Glasgow is giving in to the thugs. Certainly there have been some problems over the years at these fixtures, but by and large, they have been happy events. Football, particularly in this case, is the excuse and not the cause. If it was to do with transport and the Bank Holiday date then why wasn't something done earlier? The timing of the decision smacks of political sensationalism.

Banning alcohol sounds sensible – to the outsider! Selling drink to a football crowd is nothing more than an amenity these days and hardly a profit-making venture. Football grounds are the wrong places to go for a drink. For a start most punters arrive half an hour before the kick-off when, by the time they have queued at the bar they are likely to spill more than they drink amid a jostling crowd.

I listened with great interest to the Chief Constable of Liverpool soon after the Chelsea and Millwall events and he remarked that if supporters want to get drunk they will do so before they get to the game and that no one gets drunk once at a football ground. The Chief Constable, who has great experience of large football crowds, also said that he believed fencing in supporters was also wrong because if people are treated like animals they will behave like animals and that segregation and fencing only provide an all too obvious target for darts and other missiles. He spoke a great deal of common sense and I believe that if a group of Chief Constables from the major cities could form a committee every year, along with responsible football officials, they could lay down guidelines to reduce the possibility of violence breaking out. I say reduce because the laws of average indicate that when a large group of young people gather there is certain to be some unrest. These people are not football hooligans, just hooligans who ride on the back of football. An annual meeting would be necessary because even hooliganism changes and the problems of two years ago are not the problems of today.

There are certain clubs that do number this hooligan element among their following. They, and everyone in football, know who they are without spelling out a list of names and when they are on the rampage then everyone has to be very, very careful. This is where the experience of the Chief Constables would be so useful and their guidelines could be used by those clubs and towns who rarely suffer the excesses of this type of violence.

It was suggested that there were some dark forces involved in the riots at Kenilworth Road when the visiting Millwall fans continually spilled over the boundary walls and onto the pitch, fighting with rival fans and police alike. Millwall are undoubtedly one of those clubs high on the danger list and this was one of those instances when co-operation between two police forces might have helped prevent the trouble. The Bedfordshire police clearly underestimated the number of visiting fans who would make the journey down the M1 or take the short commuter train ride from St Pancras, but if the Metropolitan Police had monitored the numbers they might have been able to warn the police in Luton that many more than anticipated were on their way. At the other end of the scale, Crystal Palace had a relegation match against Notts County on Easter Monday last season attended by less than 5000 supporters with only 100 or so visiting fans making the trip, yet we had dozens of police including mounted officers which was a clear case of overkill. In the instance of those Millwall followers they needed protection from themselves and far from it being a politically-motivated riot it looked to me like a small mindless group of lunatics out to make a name for themselves.

So, what do we do? I believe that the Government could help in a far more concrete way if they drafted bills that defined acts of hooliganism as basically modern criminal offences. The laws should cover not just those who cause trouble at football matches but also those who commit similar acts at demonstrations, marches and carnivals. For too long we have heard magistrates say that they can only hand out sentences or fines in accordance with the charges laid before them while the police also feel that they are tied down by the laws under which they operate. Because they are called football supporters, hooligans get away with a fine or a few hours' community service. This is wrong. They are behaving criminally and should be treated as such. The Government should give the police the powers to make the proper charges and the magistrates the authority to put the villains away for a long time. In any other situation, someone who threw a dart or a Stanley blade would be considered an animal and treated like one. Let us call these people by their right name, football has no part in it. They are no better than criminals and if they caused trouble anywhere else that is how they would be branded.

Not so obvious to the casual observer, but an area which I feel particularly strongly about from my own experience, is the standard of medical care available for players which, in this country, sadly falls short of the examples set in Scandinavia and the United States. Most sportsmen and women will be able to relate tales of visiting their local general practitioner or the casualty ward of a hospital and being treated at both with scant regard, almost as if their injuries had been self inflicted and they were frowned upon for wasting time which could have been devoted to accident victims and the like. The medical facilities available have improved in recent years but not nearly enough. I would like to see every club with a qualified physiotherapist on their staff and with specialists more readily available. Even a huge outfit like Liverpool does not employ a qualified physiotherapist, preferring to send their injured players to specialists. How much better if they had men on the spot like American grid iron football teams who are able to make an instant diagnosis even during the game.

Of course it means an added expense to already hard-up clubs but surely the fitness of their players is of crucial importance. The situation is improving gradually with sports clinics being set up in various parts of the country. But how can an out-of-work parks footballer afford that? A far more practical solution would be for the Football Association to investigate ways of providing treatment for their members; after all there are 40,000 affiliated clubs paying dues and medical care would give them something really tangible for their money. If there are not sufficient funds then perhaps a sponsor could be found, someone like Smith and Nephew whose products are included in every football club's medical kit. What an advertisement it would be for them with more than 50,000 grateful patients.

The centres are ready-made at the 92 professional football clubs who would be performing a valuable service to the community. In the past the International Athletes Club's former secretary David Bedford, himself forced to quit his chosen sport because of injury, negotiated for most of the League Clubs to offer their physiotherapy and medical facilities to our international athletes while my own experience at Old Trafford was that Jim McGregor was always ready to help out other sportsmen or dancers who were struggling with injury.

It might also lead to greater control and more information about the use of painkillers. I admit to having steroid injections and taking drugs to allow me to play in an important match but, as I have said before, it has always been my decision totally with no pressure whatsoever from my manager. It is left up to the player to be strong enough to say no and, as I discovered, it is not always easy. There are so many factors such as not wanting to miss a big game, bonuses and worries over whether you will regain your place. When my knee was causing me a great deal of pain, Jim McGregor took me quietly to one side one day shortly before a big game, gave me a pill and whispered 'Take this, it will help you.' I took it without any questions and it was only later he told me that it was a placebo, nothing more than a sugar-coated aspirin designed to do more for the mind than the body.

You often hear stories about drug use in sport but I have had little experience of it in the British game, though we know it happens from the unfortunate incident involving Willie Johnston in the Argentina 1978 World Cup Finals. While we may not have the medical facilities available to the American Grid Iron teams, neither do we have their drug problem. Responsible American sports magazines have reported the increasing use of hashish and cocaine among their footballers and sprinters, even to snorting other powdered drugs off their sweatbands. They are used by those who need a burst of power in an event which needs no great control. I would doubt, for example, that a quarter-back would take anything that could cloud his judgement.

Much the same applies to footballers and stimulants. I cannot see the value in training all week under normal conditions and then taking a stimulant that allows for misjudgements which could see a player heft the ball into touch rather than cross it to the far post.

I discussed the use of stimulants with a group of experts who said that a footballer would get as much of a lift from a cup of strong black coffee, through the caffeine content, as from the average pep pill. The Football Assocation carries out random drug tests and their findings definitely do not suggest any drug abuse at all within the game. I approve, for prevention must be better than cure and should there ever develop a problem, either with stimulants or with clubs demanding players to take pain killers, the PFA would come down like a ton of bricks.

Sadly it is inevitable that, at the end of a career dotted with injuries, there are going to be after effects and while I was at the PFA I saw plenty of older players suffering from complaints like arthritis, men who can't get about and who can't work. Only a handful are self inflicted but, even so, there is little that can be done other than providing better medical advice and treatment during their careers. Just as doctors suffer a high rate of suicide and journalists broken marriages, footballers are prone to leg injuries. It is an occupational hazard and we all know the risks when we sign that first contract.

Despite what has happened to me I have no regrets. I signed my first two-year contract simply to see me through university and look what happened to me! I cannot think of anything else that would have given me the thrills that football has. Now that football is beginning to diversify and become a competitive business I hold no fears for its future. Most important is that football is in charge of its own future and as long as the prospect of a quick buck does not dominate in the long term, then our national game will thrive. My motto has always been 'que será será', whatever will be will be and though I have had my peaks and troughs, I would not swap a minute of my football career.